UNDERSTANDING NCEA

A RELATIVELY SHORT AND VERY USEFUL GUIDE
FOR SECONDARY SCHOOL STUDENTS
AND THEIR PARENTS

2ND EDITION

IRENA MADJAR AND **ELIZABETH MCKINLEY**

Starpath Project for Tertiary Participation and Success

NZCER PRESS

Wellington 2013

NZCER PRESS
New Zealand Council for Educational Research
PO Box 3237
Wellington
New Zealand

© Irena Madjar and Elizabeth McKinley, 2013
ISBN 978-1-927231-00-5
All rights reserved

National Library of New Zealand Cataloguing-in-Publication Data
Madjar, Irena.
Understanding NCEA : a relatively short and very useful guide for secondary school students and their parents / Irena Madjar and Elizabeth McKinley (Starpath Project for Tertiary Participation and Success). 2nd edition.
ISBN 978-1-927231-00-5
1. National Certificate of Educational Achievement (New Zealand) 2. Education, Secondary—Curricula—New Zealand. 3. Vocational guidance—New Zealand. I. McKinley, Elizabeth Ann. II. Title.
373.12620993—dc 23

Designed by Cluster Creative
Illustrations by James Watson
Printed by Printlink, Wellington

This title is also available as an e-book from www.nzcer.org.nz/nzcerpress.

Distributed by NZCER
PO Box 3237
Wellington
New Zealand
www.nzcer.org.nz

CONTENTS

Acknowledgements	5
Foreword	7
Introduction	11
You need a book to understand NCEA?!	12
How this book can help you	14
1 Getting to grips with NCEA	**15**
The essential things you need to know about NCEA	16
A few other things you need to know about NCEA	23
What you need to know about the University Entrance award	26
What you need to know about the New Zealand Scholarship award	28
Key points	31
2 If science is your thing	**35**
Introduction	36
Rangi	36
Leilani	40
Jason	45
Key points	50
3 If you prefer arts and social sciences	**53**
Introduction	54
Jessica	54
Benji	58
Lucy	63
Key points	69

4	**If business and commerce is where you want to be**	73
	Introduction	74
	Jack	75
	Anna	81
	Michael	86
	Key points	92
5	**Builder, plumber, soldier, chef?**	95
	Introduction	96
	Apprenticeships	97
	Armed services	102
	Key points	111
6	**What parents can do to help**	113
	Introduction	114
	Getting started with NCEA	115
	Making NCEA work for your child	122
	Key points	130

Appendix 1   133
Curriculum flow charts

Appendix 2   139
Significant standards for progression to higher levels within core subjects of English, mathematics and science

Appendix 3   143
Useful websites and sources of further information

Glossary   149

ACKNOWLEDGEMENTS

The Starpath Project for Tertiary Participation and Success was established in 2005. Its aim is to investigate ways of transforming current patterns of educational underachievement in New Zealand secondary schools, particularly for Māori and Pacific students, and students from low- to mid-decile schools. One of the barriers to student success we identified was that many parents, students and even teachers have a poor understanding of NCEA (the National Certificates of Educational Achievement).

This book was born out of our realisation that, when it comes to NCEA, parents, students and schools are often talking past each other. Our research indicates that parents are still struggling to understand how NCEA can work for their child. Students are often left to manage their own NCEA pathways. Some do it very well indeed, but too many students work out where the short cuts might be (such as how to get the most credits for the least effort), without appreciating the longer term consequences of their decisions.

Hence this book! In it we have drawn on our research and written specifically for students and parents—not for academics or researchers (unless they are also parents still trying to work out the ins and outs of NCEA). All the stories in the book are based on our research, but in each case we have combined a number of stories, changed names and other identifying details, and added a few elements to make the material easier to understand.

This book would not have been possible without the heartfelt stories told to us by many students and parents who took part in our research.

We thank them for giving us the material from which to write, and the reason for writing. If other students and their parents, new to NCEA, find this book useful we will have achieved our goal.

This second edition of the book was made necessary by a number of changes to the NCEA regulations over the past 2 years, including those related to numeracy and literacy and the University Entrance requirements.

We are grateful to the Starpath partner schools who continue to teach us about the realities and challenges of educating our young people. Thank you to the Starpath research team, and in particular Seini Jensen, who undertook many of the parent and student interviews and ensured we heard the stories we needed to hear.

We also acknowledge all those who have provided suggestions and feedback on the initial drafts of this book—in particular, Dr Samantha Smith for her intellectual input and clarifying comments; Mr Michael Withiel for his thorough and insightful critique; Shona Ramsay, Senior Policy Analysis at NZQA; and the many anonymous students and parents for their comments and suggestions.

The curriculum flow charts in Appendix 1 are reproduced with the permission of Kaitaia College, and we thank the school for allowing us to use this material.

Finally, we thank David Ellis, publishing manager at NZCER Press, for championing the book and helping us, expertly and patiently, through the sometimes intricate publication process, and James Watson for his quirky but brilliant illustrations.

Irena Madjar and Elizabeth McKinley
Starpath Project (www.starpath.auckland.ac.nz)
The University of Auckland
July 2013

FOREWORD

NCEA can seem like a mystery for those who are new to it. Many parents experienced a system where they were asked to study all year and then sit exams at the end (usually in the gym or the hall). They would then wait for their results to come in the mail, during January, to reveal whether they had succeeded or not. A whole year's work depended on a few exams!

This is not how NCEA works. Since NCEA was introduced in 2002 it has been reviewed and improved and has become New Zealand's main qualification system for secondary school students. But it is not as straightforward as the exam-based qualifications.

There were good reasons for introducing NCEA. The nature and range of jobs have changed since parents were at school, tertiary education no longer depends solely on end-of-year exams, and there are many more tertiary courses to choose from. This means that today's students need to be prepared differently.

Think of the modern workplace: the job performance review is based on many things that occurred during the past year and not on one single task. During the year an employee will be asked to complete many tasks, learn new things and put these into practice. This is the same with NCEA: there are many ways to learn new things (via credits and courses), many ways to put these into practice (internal and external assessments), and multiple ways for performance to be valued (Excellent, Merit, Achieved). As in the average workplace (and certainly when learning challenging material), there may also be more than one opportunity to succeed in a task.

However, this flexibility of NCEA comes with complexity, which can lead to many questions. This book aims to provide many of the answers and to help you identify which questions to ask. It is based on a number of years of research in schools—interviewing students, teachers and parents, analysing patterns and results, and publishing many articles. The complexity of NCEA means there can be "chokepoints": points where poor decisions are made that can have negative consequences on students' aspirations. It could be that the school does not offer the optimal balance of courses for the student to choose from. Students could be aiming too low and choosing the easier subjects, which may later prevent access to desired courses. Or students and families may not be planning a sequence through NCEA. This book will be invaluable for addressing these and many other chokepoints, and the questions that arise from them.

The Starpath team is the foremost research group on NCEA, analysing the effects in schools and the effects of NCEA on students when they move beyond the school gates into tertiary study, the workplace and other destinations. One of the more exciting findings is that performance in NCEA is among the world's best predictors of success in later studies. This is because NCEA requires that students learn to study *throughout* the year, complete assignments to specified standards, and learn continually from these assignments how to improve their work. Their performance is assessed across many pieces of work and not just one test on one day of the year. This is how university and most workplaces now operate.

I encourage parents and students to use this book as a source of information and a point of discussion, to work through the examples seeing how the courses are put together and, most importantly, know what questions to ask your school. Don't leave the school out of the questioning—they are keen to help answer your queries—and after reading this book you are more likely to have the right questions to ask them.

Professor John Hattie
Formerly of the Faculty of Education
The University of Auckland

INTRODUCTION

Once upon a time students turned up at school and teachers decided what they needed to learn, how they should be taught, and what grades or qualifications they had earned. Today things are very different, especially when it comes to senior high school years and the National Certificates of Educational Achievement (NCEA). NCEA is the national school leaving qualification, used by the majority of secondary schools in New Zealand. It allows students to choose from a large number of subjects, to decide how much content they wish to learn and, to a certain extent, to decide how they wish to be assessed.

Under the pre-2002 system, students who failed to achieve School Certificate or a higher qualification came away with a failed record. Achievement depended entirely on the end-of-year exam results for each subject, and national results were adjusted so that only half of the students passed.

The NCEA system, introduced in 2002 and used during the final 3 years of secondary schooling, is different in several ways.

- Students' learning is assessed both during and at the end of the school year.

- Assessment is "standards based". In other words, if a student achieves a set standard for a particular section of a subject or course, he or she is awarded a pass, regardless of how any other students performed.

- Students' Records of Achievement document what the students have learned and what skills they have mastered, for all the courses they have undertaken.

NCEA is offered at three levels: Level 1 (usually in Year 11), Level 2 (usually in Year 12) and Level 3 (usually in Year 13). A particular combination of subjects, mostly at Level 3, makes up the University Entrance (UE) qualification.

On the surface, then, NCEA can seem simple and straight forward. So, why do we think that students and their families might find this book useful when dealing with NCEA for the first time, such as at the end of Year 10, when students are choosing subjects for NCEA Level 1 in Year 11? And why might it also be helpful to students further along the NCEA path?

YOU NEED A BOOK TO UNDERSTAND NCEA?!

The main reason we wrote this book was because NCEA is both complex and flexible, and that can make it difficult to understand for people who are new to it. Our aim is to make NCEA understandable, so that students and their families can make NCEA work for them and help them reach their goals. This is especially important for students aiming to go on to tertiary education, including university.

NCEA is complex

NCEA is complex because it is designed to meet the needs of students with a broad range of abilities and interests. It can accommodate students who need to prepare for university studies in medicine or engineering, those who plan to undertake apprenticeships in building or hairdressing, as well as those who want to learn mostly practical skills and join the workforce directly from school. This means that a large high school might offer 40 or more subjects, from accounting to woodwork. Because each student is able to take only five or six subjects each year, how do you decide which subjects to take?

To make things more difficult, many subjects have prerequisites. This means that to be allowed to do music, or French, at Level 3 (Year 13), for example, a student needs to have done these subjects at Levels 1 (Year 11) and 2 (Year 12). Sometimes schools will allow a student to go on without a specified prerequisite, but in most cases the expectation is that the prerequisites listed in the school curriculum guide will be met. How does a student at the end of Year 10 know what he or she will want to study 3 years later?

NCEA is flexible

Because it is designed to meet the needs of students with different interests and abilities, NCEA is flexible. This means that:

- schools can select which standards (components) to include in a subject and can adjust subject content to suit the learning needs of their students

- students can study catering along with physics, and many other combinations of subjects

- students can study at different Levels of NCEA at the same time, even within the same subjects or courses

- students can complete non-NCEA subjects and have them credited towards NCEA, and they can use NCEA credits towards other (non-NCEA) qualifications.

This flexibility also means that schools can offer different versions of core subjects such as English, maths and science—some designed for "academically able" students going on to university, and others for students thought to need a more "practical" or "applied" knowledge of these subjects.

HOW THIS BOOK CAN HELP YOU

NCEA's complexity and flexibility can be a trap for students without clear goals, good advice, and careful planning. We hope this book will help you become more informed about how NCEA works, and how you can make it work for you. The first chapter outlines how NCEA works. It is intended primarily for students, but it is important that parents read it too.

The final chapter is written specially for parents/whānau and explains why it is important that, as parents, you talk with your children (and their teachers) about their subject choices, how well they are doing at school, and what they hope to do when they leave school. To help your children you need to understand what they are doing, when you can stand back, and when it might be a good idea to step in and talk with them or their school.

Chapters 2, 3, 4 and 5 are based on stories of students making different kinds of subject choices, some helpful, some not. Based on real-life experiences of over 120 students we have talked with in the course of our research, these stories show how students can plan their pathways through the three NCEA years and what can happen when they make good (or not so good) choices. Individual names are made up, and the stories are based on a whole collection of different stories and do not describe specific individuals.

A list of useful websites for further information is provided at the end of the book.

1
GETTING TO GRIPS WITH NCEA

NCEA is a national school leaver qualification that fits within the larger New Zealand Qualifications Framework. Most of the subjects offered by secondary schools in New Zealand are based on the Learning Areas in the New Zealand Curriculum (which provides a framework for what secondary schools are expected to teach). Some schools also offer unit standards in other subjects, such as business administration or animal care, that are not part of the New Zealand Curriculum but can earn credits towards both NCEA and other (non-NCEA) qualifications.

Before choosing any subject, you need to know how it will help you achieve at school and how well it will prepare you for further education or work after school.

THE ESSENTIAL THINGS YOU NEED TO KNOW ABOUT NCEA

Standards and credits

Secondary schools offer subjects made up of **standards** (subject components) that are assessed to meet the NCEA requirements.

Each standard carries a certain number of points or **credits** (typically between 2 and 6) that are awarded when you satisfy the assessment for that standard.

A subject such as Level 1 English might be made up of anywhere from 4 or 5 to 10 or more standards, which can allow you to earn as many as 24 or more credits. For example, a standard might require that you produce examples of formal writing such as a job application, and carry 3 credits; another standard might require that you create and deliver a speech, and carry a further 3 credits.

If you do not submit required work or sit the required test or exam for a particular standard, you will not earn any credits for *that* standard, but you can still earn credits for *other* standards in the same subject.

Don't be tempted to skip standards that carry only 2 or 3 credits; the content could be very important.

Schools usually offer two types of standards: **achievement standards**, which come from the New Zealand Curriculum (in subjects such as history, chemistry, maths, or English), and **unit standards**, which usually come from other qualifications such as hospitality, technology, or business administration.

Assessment and grades

- In place of traditional A, B, C, D grades, NCEA credits are awarded as **Not Achieved** (N), **Achieved** (A), **Merit** (M) or **Excellence** (E). Achievement standards are assessed using all four grades. In most cases unit standards are assessed using only the Achieved and Not Achieved grades.

- Some assessments (including all unit standard assessments) are done internally, during the school year, by the teachers teaching the subjects. Other assessments are done externally (through exams or portfolios), at the end of the school year, by specially appointed examiners. Subjects are often made up of a combination of internally and externally assessed standards, allowing students to earn some credits during the year and additional credits through end-of-year external assessments.

- If a student *fails to achieve a standard or a set of standards* that are internally assessed, there is usually one further opportunity to resubmit written work or be reassessed for it. For externally assessed standards there is only one opportunity to achieve the standard—at the end of the school year. (A second attempt would have to wait until the end of the following year.)

Ensuring the system works fairly

NCEA is managed by the New Zealand Qualifications Authority (NZQA), which also approves and monitors other qualifications on the New Zealand Qualifications Framework. NZQA ensures that schools maintain similar standards of internal assessment, by a process called moderation. This involves a sample of students' work already assessed by a teacher being sent for assessment by an external teacher (a moderator) so that standards of assessment across different schools can be compared. Feedback is provided so that, if necessary, teachers can adjust their marking criteria for future use to indicate results that are similar to those provided by teachers from most other schools.

Achieving NCEA Level 1

Most students start to study for NCEA in Year 11 (5th form in the old system), although it is possible to start in Year 10 or even earlier, especially in areas such as music performance, te reo Māori or other languages in which a student is achieving well already.

> IT IS UP TO YOU TO DECIDE HOW HARD YOU WANT TO WORK AND WHICH ASSESSMENTS YOU WANT TO ATTEMPT.

In **Year 11** you will be required to take five or six subjects. This depends on the school and the school timetable. English (or te reo Māori) and maths (or pāngarau) are compulsory in almost all schools at this level. Some schools add a third compulsory subject. Usually it is science, but it might be physical education or another subject.

You are free to choose the remaining subjects, but your choice might be restricted by which subjects are available in your school, how the timetable is organised, and how well you have done on various tests and assessments the previous year. Potentially, you will be given the opportunity to earn 120 or more credits across five or six subjects. It is up to you to decide how hard you want to work and which assessments you want to attempt.

To gain **NCEA Level 1** you will need to earn:

- a *total* of at least **80 credits**, including
- at least **10 credits showing *literacy* skills**
- at least **10 credits showing *numeracy* skills**

Literacy credits are intended to demonstrate your reading, writing, speaking and listening skills. They can be earned through either:

- Specified Achievement Standards available through a range of subjects (such as English, te reo Māori, history, or social studies), OR
- Specified Unit Standards. These come as a package of three standards, together worth 10 credits, and all three must be completed successfully to meet the literacy requirement.

Note that you have to meet the literacy requirements through either specified Achievement Standards or the specified Unit Standards, but not a mix of the two.

There is one further way to meet the literacy requirements and that is through a special Level 4 subject called English for Academic Purposes. This subject is made up of two Unit Standards each worth five credits. Students taking this option may choose to achieve both reading and writing credits through this subject, or to achieve only reading or writing this way and to achieve the other part through specified Achievement Standards.

Numeracy credits are intended to demonstrate your number, measurement, and statistical skills. They can be earned through either:

- Specified Achievement Standards available through a range of subjects (such as maths, pāngarau, geography, or science), OR

- Specified Unit Standards. These come as a package of three standards, together worth 10 credits, and all three must be completed successfully to meet the numeracy requirement.

Note that you have to meet the numeracy requirements through either specified Achievement Standards or the specified Unit Standards, but not a mix of the two.

Your school will help to ensure that you are enrolled in appropriate standards to achieve the literacy and numeracy requirements. You can also check the full list of these on the NZQA website (http://www.nzqa.govt.nz/qualifications-standards/qualifications/ncea).

EACH YEAR OF STUDY PROVIDES THE FOUNDATION FOR THE NEXT YEAR'S WORK

Most students should aim to complete NCEA Level 1 in Year 11, and to complete more than the minimum 80 credits, especially if they are aiming to go on to tertiary education. However, the flexibility of NCEA allows students to take Level 1 subjects in Years 12 and 13, and some students might need the extra time. You do not have to complete NCEA Level 1 to be allowed to take Level 2 subjects and complete NCEA Level 2, but it is better if you do. Conversely, you could take some higher-level standards in Year 11, especially if you are doing well in particular subjects and your teachers think you are ready for more advanced study.

Overall, each year of study provides the foundation for the next year's work, and it is much easier to do well if you have a solid foundation on which to build at each new level of learning. In Appendix 1, at the end of the book, we have included a flow chart that shows how subjects in earlier years connect to what students can do in later years. The flow charts come from one school and are provided as an example only. Your school will have similar charts (usually included in a Curriculum Guide or NCEA Subject Handbook) that will list all the subjects available at your school and show how specific subjects are connected from Years 10 or 11 through to Year 13.

Achieving NCEA Level 2

In most schools in **Year 12** you will be required to take English (or te reo Māori). Many schools require their students to also take maths (or pāngarau) at this level. The choice of the optional three or four subjects is very important at this point. Level 1 maths and science serve as prerequisites for subjects such as statistics, physics, chemistry and biology. Good performance in Level 1 English can also act as a prerequisite for subjects such as drama, media studies or social studies. But prerequisites become stricter for Level 3, so you need to think carefully about the subjects you might like to take in Year 12, and also whether these subjects will allow you to study what you might want (or need) to study in Year 13. (See Appendix 2 for further details about specific standards that are important for progression to higher-level studies.)

To gain **NCEA Level 2** you will need to earn:

- at least **60 credits** at Level 2 or above, and another **20 credits** at any other level (these 20 credits can come from already-earned Level 1 credits).

- From 2013, you must also meet the Level 1 literacy and numeracy requirements.

Although it might seem that NCEA Level 2 is easier to achieve than Level 1 (because fewer credits are required), the material you will be studying will be at a higher academic level, so you will need to step up to the challenge. Again, making the most of what you are able to learn at Level 2 will help you to be well prepared for the following year. Note that you might be able to progress to NCEA Level 2 study, even if you did not achieve NCEA Level 1 the previous year. But, if you did not achieve the literacy or numeracy requirements you will need to do so before you can be awarded NCEA Level 2.

Remember that this is the minimum requirement. Most students can, and do, earn more than 60 Level 2 credits. This is important for two reasons:

- You are required to take five or six subjects, each with 20 or more credits, so you should be making the most of the opportunities to learn as much as you can in each of these subjects.
- You need to make sure that you achieve enough credits in each subject to meet the "subject pass" or prerequisite rule at your school, so that you are able to study these subjects at a more advanced level in Year 13. Schools usually require at least 12, and often as many as 16 to 18 credits, for a subject pass at this level.

If you are thinking about going to university when you leave school, instead of relying on the already-earned Level 1 credits, you should be aiming to achieve at least 80 or more Level 2 credits.

Achieving NCEA Level 3

In **Year 13** you will be free to choose all your subjects, but remember that your choices will be limited by the prerequisites you have completed in previous years. If you are aiming to go to university, check carefully which subjects are required for the programme you wish to study. Also, make sure that the subjects you take count not only towards NCEA Level 3 but also towards the UE award.

To gain **NCEA Level 3** you will need to earn:

- at least **60 credits** at Level 3 or above, and another **20 credits** at Level 2 or higher (these 20 credits can come from already-earned Level 2 credits).

Any NCEA Level 3 subjects (and some non-NCEA Level 3 subjects[1]) can contribute credits toward the NCEA Level 3 qualification, but not all Level 3 subjects count towards UE.

A FEW OTHER THINGS YOU NEED TO KNOW ABOUT NCEA

NCEA is designed to meet the learning needs of all students in many different subjects and with varying interests and levels of ability. Each student's Record of Achievement will document the knowledge and skills attained and the credits earned in the process. Every achievement (and every recorded credit) counts and will show on your Record of Achievement.

Why is achieving NCEA important?

All students should be able to leave school with useful knowledge and skills, preferably with a formal qualification. NCEA Level 1 is the minimum school leaving qualification, although current policy is that the majority of students should leave school with at least NCEA Level 2. Achieving an NCEA qualification is important for many reasons. Here are some of the most important:

- Students who move from school to the workforce with an NCEA qualification have a higher chance of getting a job and being paid a higher wage than those who leave without a qualification. How much a person can earn is closely related to their level of education.

- Students who wish to take up an apprenticeship are usually required to have achieved certain levels of literacy and numeracy as well

---

1 As already mentioned, school subjects with achievement standards are part of the secondary schools curriculum. Other subjects can come from other certificate or diploma qualifications on the New Zealand Qualifications Framework. Such subjects might include workshop skills, animal care or business administration, and there are many others.

as other skills (see Chapter 5 for some examples). Those with an NCEA Level 2 qualification are much more likely to complete their apprenticeships and become qualified builders, motor mechanics, plumbers, etc. than those without this qualification.

- Students who want to complete certificate or diploma courses (in technology, business, landscape gardening, aged care or other fields) through industry training organisations, polytechnics or other training providers are generally expected to have completed NCEA Level 2, or a significant number of credits toward NCEA Level 2, particularly in literacy and numeracy.

- Entry to degree-level studies at polytechnics usually requires UE or NCEA Level 3. Where the requirements for entry are less demanding (e.g., for diploma courses), strong performance at NCEA Level 2 is expected.

- Entry to university degree-level programmes requires a minimum of UE and a significant number of credits in subjects on the **approved list** (see Chapters 2, 3 and 4 for examples). In fact, some universities are now using a point system to rank students for selection into specific degree programmes. The points are usually calculated on the basis of Level 3 approved subjects, with extra points for credits achieved with Merit or Excellence (see Jack's story in Chapter 4 for an example of how the point system might work).

Although some students will settle for the minimum effort needed to achieve their NCEA qualifications (or less), many more students will be keen to do their best and achieve as much as possible. NCEA rewards hard work and academic achievement through course and certificate endorsements. Students who achieve credits with Merit or Excellence may qualify for endorsement.

Course endorsement

Course endorsement (e.g., in te reo Māori, chemistry or French) requires that a student achieve at least 14 credits in that subject with Merit or Excellence. At least 3 of the 14 credits must come from internal assessment and at least 3 credits from external assessment (except in the case of physical education, religious studies and Level 3 visual arts). The credits can come from more than one NCEA Level, but they must all be earned in the same school year.

For example, a student who achieves 20 credits in Level 2 chemistry (4 from internal and 16 from external assessments), 15 of which are achieved with Excellence, will gain endorsement in chemistry "with Excellence". Another student, with the same number of credits and proportions of internal and external assessment, but who achieves 10 credits with Merit and 4 with Excellence (some of these credits at Level 1 and others at Level 2), will gain endorsement in chemistry "with Merit".

Check with your school that the subjects you are taking, and hope to achieve with Merit or Excellence, have been structured so that they are eligible for endorsement.

Certificate endorsement

Certificate endorsement (at NCEA Levels 1, 2 or 3) requires that a student achieve at least 50 credits towards a certificate with Merit or Excellence. For example, a student completing NCEA Level 2 who achieves a total of 96 Level 2 credits, 52 of which are with Excellence, will be awarded NCEA Level 2 "with Excellence". A student who achieves 64 Level 2 credits, 20 of them with Excellence and 31 with Merit, will be awarded NCEA Level 2 "with Merit".

WHAT YOU NEED TO KNOW ABOUT THE UNIVERSITY ENTRANCE AWARD

To achieve **University Entrance (UE)**, usually in Year 13, you will need to meet a different set of requirements than for NCEA Level 3. Not all NCEA Level 3 subjects count towards UE. The ones that do are on the **approved list of subjects**, as shown in Table 1 below.[2] And just to make things even more complicated, not all standards within the approved list of subjects count towards UE, so check with your school that the standards being offered do count.

Achieving UE from 2014

To achieve UE students are required to:

- **achieve NCEA Level 3** (i.e., at least 60 credits at Level 3 or above and 20 credits at Level 2 or above, including Level 2 credits completed in previous years)

- **achieve at least 14 credits** in each of at least three subjects on the approved list (i.e., at least 42 credits from the three subjects)—these credits are part of the 60 credits required for NCEA Level 3

- **meet the literacy requirement** of at least **10 credits** in English, te reo Māori, or other specified achievement or unit standards at Level 2 or above (5 of which must be in reading/panui and 5 in writing/tuhituhi)

- **meet the numeracy requirement** of at least **10 credits** at Level 1 or above in mathematics, pāngarau, or other specified achievement or unit standards (the numeracy requirement for UE is the same as the numeracy requirement for NCEA Level 1).

---

2 As listed on the NZQA website on 5 June 2013. For changes and updates, check at http://www.nzqa.govt.nz/qualifications-standards/awards/university-entrance/approved-subjects/

Table 1: The list of approved subjects for UE from 2014

ART AND DESIGN
Design (Practical Art)
Design & Visual Communication
Painting (Practical Art)
Photography (Practical Art)
Printmaking (Practical Art)
Sculpture (Practical Art)

HUMANITIES AND SOCIAL SCIENCES
Classical Studies
Dance
Drama
Geography
History
History of Art
Media Studies
Music Studies
Religious Studies
Social Studies

BUSINESS AND COMMERCE
Accounting
Business Studies
Economics

LANGUAGES AND LITERATURE
Cook Island Māori
Chinese
English
French
German
Indonesian
Japanese
Korean
Latin
Samoan
Spanish
Te Reo Māori
Te Reo Rangatira

SCIENCE
Agriculture & Horticulture
Biology
Chemistry
Earth & Space Science
Physics
Science

MATHEMATICS
Calculus
Mathematics
Statistics

OTHER SUBJECTS
Construction & Mechanical Technologies
Digital Technologies
Education for Sustainability
Health Education
Home Economics
Physical Education
Processing Technologies
Technology

Students with a strong academic record at school (Merit and Excellence endorsements) tend to do better at university than students who did less well at school. So you should make the most of your final year at school and gain NCEA Level 3 and UE, with as many Merits and Excellences as possible!

It is important you make sure that the subjects you are taking at Level 3, and expect to be counted towards UE, are on the approved list, and that the majority (if not all) the standards within these subjects are also included on the approved list. Similarly, if you are aiming for course and certificate endorsements, make sure that the courses you are taking are eligible for endorsement.

WHAT YOU NEED TO KNOW ABOUT THE NEW ZEALAND SCHOLARSHIP AWARD

There is one additional level of academic award available to senior high school students, called the **New Zealand Scholarship award.** This award is given to students who can show very high levels of achievement in individual subjects. Students are assessed on the basis of external end-of-year examinations or portfolios (covering the same content but separate from external assessments for NCEA), and carry a monetary reward which is available only when the student enrols in tertiary study in New Zealand. Scholarships are awarded at the basic Scholarship (S) level, or the Outstanding (O) level.

> STUDENTS WITH A STRONG ACADEMIC RECORD AT SCHOOL (MERIT AND EXCELLENCE GRADES) ALSO TEND TO DO BETTER AT UNIVERSITY THAN STUDENTS WHO DID LESS WELL AT SCHOOL

Scholarship awards (and their 2012 monetary values) are as follows:

- *Single Subject Award*: $500 (one-off)—for one subject (or $1,000 for achievement in two Scholarship subjects). In 2012, 2038 students received this award.

- *Scholarship Award*: $2,000 per year for 3 years, as long as the student maintains at least a B grade average in tertiary studies—for achievement in three or more Scholarship subjects. In 2012, 224 students received this award.

- *Top Subject Scholarship Award*: $2,000 per year for 3 years, as long as the student maintains at least a B grade average in tertiary studies—for achieving the highest marks in a subject. In 2012 there were 33 Top Subject Scholarship winners.

- *Outstanding Scholar Award*: $5,000 per year for 3 years, as long as the student maintains at least a B grade average in tertiary studies—for achieving at least two subject Scholarships at O level and at least one at S level, *or* one at O level and at least four at S level. The number of students who receive this award is restricted, and achieving the minimum number of S and O levels does not guarantee an award. Between 40 and 60 students across New Zealand achieve this award each year. In 2012 there were 54 winners.

- *Premier Award:* $10,000 per year for 3 years, as long as the student maintains at least a B grade average in tertiary studies—for achieving five or more Scholarships with at least three at O level. The number of students who receive this award is restricted, and achieving the minimum number of S and O levels does not guarantee an award. Between five and 10 Premier Awards are given out each year. In 2012 there were 10 winners.

Sitting Scholarship exams is recommended for students who have a strong record of academic excellence in one or more subjects. Winning one of the Scholarship awards is not only financially rewarding, but is also recognition of a student's academic ability and willingness to respond to a challenge. In some degree programmes, a Scholarship award in a subject can gain direct entry to second-year study in that subject.

Discuss your plans to sit Scholarship exams with your subject teachers so that they will be aware of your need to prepare for them and will help you with additional tutoring or trial runs. It is to your advantage to attempt at least three Scholarship exams, because achievement in two subjects carries a once-off award of $1,000, whereas achievement in three subjects is worth a total of $6,000 (over 3 years).

A note of clarification: New Zealand Scholarship awards should not be confused with other grants and scholarships available to students going on to tertiary studies. Many charitable organisations, community trusts, and business and service organisations offer financial assistance in the form of scholarships to students who apply for them. Universities also administer a range of scholarships and provide some of their own.

Such scholarships are often targeted at specific categories of students (e.g., women, those who come from a specific geographical area or who attended specified schools) and might be linked to specific areas of study (e.g., arts, music, engineering). Scholarships are awarded on the basis of academic achievement and other qualities, including leadership and community contribution. Some are linked to financial need. Your school and the university you plan to attend will be able to give you more information about the scholarships for which you can apply.

KEY POINTS

- Whatever your plans are for when you leave school, make sure you understand how NCEA works and how it affects your options and choices.
- Plan early where you want to go so that you can select the best possible pathway through NCEA that will get you there. Just hoping to become a teacher, lawyer, film maker or chef is not enough. To be able to get to a career of your choice it is important that you, and your parents/whānau, learn what you need to achieve at school, and how you can best achieve the required credits in the most appropriate subjects.
- As well as understanding NCEA, make sure you also understand the school "rules" that go with it. What prerequisites do you need to have, how many credits do you need to achieve, and how well do you need to do to be able to progress to the next level of a subject?
- Be aware of timetabling issues. If chemistry and tourism are timetabled in the same period, decide carefully which is more important and which you will need as a prerequisite for the following year.

- If you are not clear about your career plans, keep your options open. This usually means taking English, maths and science in Years 11 and 12, and adding one or more academic subjects.
- Whatever your aspirations or plans, do your best to achieve as much as you can while you are at school.

If your plans include university study

- Choose your NCEA subjects carefully, and try to achieve a good balance between science subjects (including maths) and subjects such as English, history, drama, social studies, media studies and classics, which will help develop your analytical and critical thinking skills as well as your writing and presentation skills.
- Aim for a good balance between essential academic studies and extracurricular activities, including sports and leadership roles. You need to develop as a rounded person, but don't allow extracurricular activities to limit your academic achievement.
- Talk with your teachers, career guidance counsellors, parents and other adults who can help you make the best possible decisions at each step through NCEA. It is really disappointing when students reach Year 13 and only then realise that they should have taken a different subject, or achieved 10 more credits in Year 11.
- Aim to achieve NCEA Level 1 in Year 11 and NCEA Level 2 in Year 12, and aim to achieve more than 60 Level 2 credits in Year 12.
- Aim to achieve both NCEA Level 3 and UE with best possible grades, and more than the minimum number of credits at this level. Universities have started using ranking procedures to select students, not only for the limited-entry degrees such as medicine or engineering, but for admission to all university degree programmes. This is also important for students planning to complete a conjoint degree (i.e., to study for two degrees at the same time, such as business and law, or economics and political science). Aim to achieve at least 18 credits in each of the subjects. How many credits

you achieve, and how many of these are with Merit or Excellence, could make the difference between acceptance in or rejection from a course and/or university of your choice.
- Consider taking the Scholarship award exams at the end of Year 13, and discuss with your teachers how you can best prepare for them.
- Check the entry requirements for the degree programme and university you plan to attend, and make sure you meet these criteria. If these include a subject your school is not offering (e.g., Level 3 physics or calculus), discuss with your school (and your parents) how you can best access that subject. Distance education, with some local support, might be one option, but it will require good time management and determination on your part.
- Review your plans, achievements, subject choices and study practices regularly to make sure you remain on track and are achieving the required targets along the way. It is especially helpful if your school is using a system of academic counselling or coaching so that you have a teacher who is aware of your plans and can help you with review and advice.

2
IF SCIENCE IS YOUR THING

INTRODUCTION

So you want to be a pharmacist, or build bridges that can withstand earthquakes, or work as a physiotherapist, veterinarian, computer engineer or chemist? Perhaps you want to design elegant buildings that are also energy efficient, or you are fascinated by numbers and would like to be a maths teacher. There are lots of possibilities out there for young people with a strong background in science and maths, but you need to plan carefully how to get there. The road through the 3 years of NCEA will not always guarantee that you will be able to follow your preferred subject choices unless *you* take control.

In this chapter we will show you what can happen, and what's helpful or not so helpful about the different pathways NCEA provides, by looking at three students interested in science.

RANGI

When he was 11, Rangi was hit by a speeding car while running to catch the school bus. He ended up in hospital with cracked ribs, a broken leg and lots of cuts and bruises. The doctors had a lot of trouble fixing his knee, and afterwards he spent many weeks having to learn to walk again. He was sore, missing his family and friends, and not all that impressed with being told what he could and couldn't do. The person who made all the difference was a lady called Jenny. She was the physiotherapist who came to see him every day and helped him to breathe and cough (even though it hurt a lot) so his lungs and ribs would heal properly. And she put him through the exercises he needed to get his knee moving so he could walk again.

Two years down the track Rangi is the local mountain bike champion and not a bad rugby player either. But he is also passionate about becoming a physiotherapist, helping other people with injuries to walk again, or helping people like his granddad's sister use their arms and legs after a stroke. It would be really awesome to specialise in sports physiotherapy and help a team like the All Blacks avoid injuries and recover quickly. You get to travel and meet interesting people all the time.

Rangi is full of dreams and plans, but he has also done his homework on what it would take to become a physiotherapist. You have to understand how the human body works, in every little detail, but you also need to know how to talk to all sorts of people and how to motivate them and get them to do things even when it's hard or it hurts a lot. (Jenny was very good at that!) Rangi started planning his NCEA pathway before he got to Year 11, and is quite clear what he needs to do at school so that in 3 years' time he will be able to enrol in a university to study physiotherapy. At his school, students are required to take five subjects and Rangi chose the following.

YEAR 11 NCEA SUBJECTS	COMMENTS
Level 1 English	Compulsory at this level. It is important to achieve literacy credits for NCEA Level 1, and to meet the prerequisites for more advanced study in English and related subjects at Level 2.
Level 1 Mathematics	Compulsory at this level. It is important to achieve numeracy credits for NCEA Level 1, and to meet the prerequisites for more advanced study in maths and related subjects at Level 2.
Level 1 Science	Compulsory at this level (at Rangi's school). This is an important prerequisite for later studies in chemistry, physics or biology.
Level 1 Te Reo Māori	Optional subject. Being Māori is important to Rangi and he wants to be able to speak te reo and be very good at it. It would also make his granddad really proud.
Level 1 Physical education	Optional subject. Rangi likes playing sport, being active and not sitting in a class all day. His friends are keen on Physical Education too, so he thought it would be fun to do one subject he could share with his mates.

Rangi could have chosen chemistry or physics or biology in place of general science. But overall he made very appropriate choices and was well prepared for the next level of study in Year 12.

YEAR 12 NCEA SUBJECTS	COMMENTS
Level 2 English	Compulsory at this level. It is important to achieve literacy credits for UE, and for the continuing development of critical thinking, writing and presentation skills.
Level 2 Mathematics	Compulsory at this level. Maths with algebra is essential preparation for more advanced study of statistics and calculus.
Level 2 Biology	Optional subject. Biology is very relevant for future study in any health-related field.
Level 2 Chemistry	Optional subject. Chemistry is very relevant for future study in any health-related field.
Level 2 Te Reo Māori	Optional subject. Rangi was keen to keep improving his proficiency in te reo.

Although Rangi continued with his sports as extracurricular activities, in Year 12 he decided to concentrate on the science subjects, to get the best possible preparation for later study in physiotherapy. For Year 13 he chose the following subjects.

YEAR 13 NCEA SUBJECTS	COMMENTS
Level 3 Statistics	This is one of the options in Level 3 maths (the other was calculus).
Level 3 Biology	This is an optional subject but one for which Rangi had the required prerequisites. It is very relevant for future study in any health-related field.
Level 3 Chemistry	This is an optional subject but one for which Rangi had the required prerequisites. It is very relevant for future study in any health-related field.

Level 3 Te Reo Māori	Knowing he would not be studying te reo at university, Rangi was keen to get one more year of formal instruction in Māori language.
Level 3 Drama	This is an optional subject Rangi chose instead of English. (Normally Level 1 and Level 2 drama would be required as prerequisites, but Rangi was given special permission to take Level 3 drama.)

That was the plan! Rangi did change his mind about one or two subjects along the way (opting for statistics rather than calculus, and drama rather than English in his final year), but he was pretty well set on a path he needed to follow. It helped that his older sister, who was studying to become a teacher, kept encouraging him to go for it. He knew that he had to get enough credits and do well each year. His aim was 20 or maybe even 24 credits in each subject, and at least half of them with Merit or Excellence. He figured there were only so many places in Year 13 classes like chemistry, or in a physiotherapy programme at university. So the better he did in each subject, the better his chances of getting in and advancing to each new level of study.

Rangi chose a fairly narrow educational path, focusing mostly on science subjects. That worked for him because he was very clear from the beginning where he wanted to go and what he needed to achieve to get there. He finished high school with 122 credits in approved subjects, quite a few with Merit and Excellence. That meant that he was prepared for a degree in physiotherapy, but also, if he wanted to, for university study in other health sciences such as pharmacy, nursing, medicine or occupational therapy. If he had changed his mind about the health science field he could still have applied to study in other areas of science such as chemistry, agriculture or even chemical engineering.

Even though it did not happen, Rangi could have had a complete change of heart and decided to study psychology, law or international business. He would not have been as well prepared in terms of specific subjects, but he could still have made a successful transition to university study. What really mattered was that he selected subjects approved for UE, worked hard, did really well at school, developed strong study skills, and gained confidence that he could achieve anything if he worked for it.

LEILANI

Born in Samoa, Leilani came to New Zealand when she was nine. Her parents wanted their four children to have better educational opportunities, so a lot was expected of Leilani. She knew she would be expected to go to university, but she was not at all clear what she wanted to study or indeed what kind of career she wanted to have. The family talk was always about how important doctors and lawyers are, but Leilani thought there had to be something else that she would be good at and enjoy doing. She was a good student, always the first to finish her homework and always keen to learn a new song or a new word (it's fun dropping a word like *peripatetic* into a conversation instead of saying that someone travels a lot, and you can annoy your brothers when you say it, without getting into trouble for it).

At the end of Year 10 Leilani had a long talk with her form teacher and the message she got loud and clear was, "Keep your options open!" If your mind (or your family) is showing you one way but your heart is far from sure about it, don't feel that you have to decide immediately. Take your time to consider different options—from florist to financial adviser, from doctor to industrial designer, from lawyer to landscape architect.

At the age of 13 or 14 very few teenagers know exactly what they want to do when they leave school, or even what they are capable of achieving if they try. That's normal, and it is OK. But it doesn't mean that you stop learning or you don't think carefully about the subjects you should be studying at school until you have figured out what you want to do with the rest of your life. The final 3 years of high school will determine how well you are prepared for the next step, whether this turns out to be work or further study. Making the best of the educational opportunities the school provides is essential. So how did Leilani rise to that challenge?

Motivation to work and study hard was not a problem. Making the right subject choices could have been. Leilani managed this by speaking with her school career guidance counsellor, double checking different options and asking her form teacher to check she was on the right track. Year 11 was not so difficult because English, maths and science were all compulsory. But she needed to make sure that her Year 10 scores did not land her in classes that sounded OK but were not on the pathway she needed to follow. She did fine in Year 10 but was not quite in the "top of the class" group.

THE FINAL 3 YEARS OF HIGH SCHOOL WILL DETERMINE HOW WELL YOU ARE PREPARED FOR THE NEXT STEP, WHETHER THIS TURNS OUT TO BE WORK OR FURTHER STUDY

From Year 11 she needed to be in the academic classes for English and maths, doing the achievement standards, having to sit quite a few external exams, and getting the skills she will need to follow the academic path that will take her to university. It might have been easier to do practical or applied maths, science or English, like some of her friends, but that would have taken her away from the path she needed to follow. This is what Leilani's first year of NCEA looked like.

YEAR 11 NCEA SUBJECTS	COMMENTS
Level 1 English	Compulsory at this level. It is important to achieve literacy credits for NCEA Level 1, and to meet the prerequisites for more advanced study in English and related subjects at Level 2.
Level 1 Mathematics	Compulsory at this level. It is important to achieve numeracy credits for NCEA Level 1, and to meet the prerequisites for more advanced study in maths and related subjects at Level 2.
Level 1 Science	Compulsory at this level (at Leilani's school). This is an important prerequisite for later studies in chemistry, physics or biology.
Level 1 History	Optional subject. History appealed to Leilani because of its focus on issues such as human rights, indigenous people and social change. It helps develop skills in information searching and evaluating evidence, and placing events into their historical and cultural contexts. It is relevant to later study of history, economics, politics, sociology or education.
Level 1 Physical education	Optional subject. Leilani likes team sports, learning about the human body and exercise, and being active. It would be relevant if she later opted to study sports science or physical education.

Having done very well in all her subjects, Leilani still needed good academic advice for the following year. She needed to make sure she kept her options open, because she had not yet decided what she wanted to study once she left school. Science was still her preferred area, but exactly what within this broad field Leilani was not sure. Her Year 12 choices were as follows.

YEAR 12 NCEA SUBJECTS	COMMENTS
Level 2 English	Compulsory at this level. It is important to achieve literacy credits for UE, and for the continuing development of critical thinking, writing and presentation skills.
Level 2 Mathematics	Compulsory at this level. Maths with algebra is also essential preparation for more advanced study of statistics and calculus.
Level 2 Physics	Optional subject. Physics is very relevant for future study in architecture, engineering, technology, medicine and other health sciences.
Level 2 Chemistry	Optional subject. Chemistry is very relevant for future study in any health-related field, nutrition, chemical engineering, technology, agriculture and food sciences.
Level 2 History	Optional subject. Leilani chose history because she enjoyed it. It also helped to keep her options open should she opt for a degree in social sciences, humanities or education.

Even at the end of Year 12 Leilani was still not sure exactly what she wanted to study at university, and that made the choice of subjects at school really important. There were quite a few attractive options, such as drama, art and design, photography and hospitality—classes Leilani would have enjoyed doing, and sharing with some of her friends. But she needed to be careful that the subjects she selected did not replace the core subjects of English, maths and sciences she needed to focus on right through her 3 NCEA years. She was able to add one fun subject every year and still made sure she kept her options open for university study later. Her Year 13 choices were as follows.

YEAR 13 NCEA SUBJECTS	COMMENTS
Level 3 English	English is important for the continuing development of critical thinking, writing and presentation skills. It also helped to keep Leilani's options open for future study.
Level 3 Calculus	This is the preferred Level 3 maths option for students going on to study sciences or engineering.
Level 3 Physics	Physics is a required subject for engineering, technology and most health sciences.
Level 3 Chemistry	Chemistry is an important subject for most science degrees, and is required for health sciences, chemical engineering, food technology and pharmacy.
Level 3 Classical studies	With a background in history and English, Leilani was able to choose this as her fifth subject. The combination of history and literature appealed to her. This is also a useful subject for degrees in law, social sciences, history, literature or arts.

One other thing that Leilani discovered was that each year the study was more demanding and she needed to put more time and effort into her homework and preparation for external exams at the end of the year. She might not have been the most gifted student at her school, but she was one of the most determined. Her chemistry, maths and physics teachers encouraged her to sit the Scholarship exams at the end of Year 13. This meant extra study and three more exams on top of the ones she was doing for NCEA. In the end she achieved Scholarship in chemistry and maths (and only just missed out on one in physics).

Leilani had thought a lot about studying to become a science teacher, or maybe a chemical engineer, but after a field visit to a university in Year 13 and talking with some students there she was ready to decide. Her choice: food technology! It was not quite what her parents had in mind, but she was keen to give it a go. It seemed to combine her fascination with science with the whole idea of food and what's in it, but in a practical way, like thinking of all the different ways of processing food to keep it fresh and tasty and easy to use. All she needed to do was convince her parents to let her leave home and move to another city, so that she could attend the university she had chosen that was offering the course she wanted to do.

With the subjects she had selected in Year 13 Leilani was well prepared to study food technology, as well as nutrition and dietetics. In fact, having received a Scholarship in chemistry she found that she did not have to do first-year chemistry at the university she had chosen for her degree studies and could take second-year chemistry instead. If she had chosen to change her direction, she would also have been able to apply for a degree in arts or social sciences (e.g., history, anthropology, psychology, sociology), in health sciences (e.g., optometry, pharmacy or nursing), or in education (teaching).

JASON

Jason had a leaning towards science and technical things. Always interested in cars and computers and the latest gadgets, Jason thought that one day he would like to work with computers, maybe even design computer games or work in the information technology (IT) field. But all that seemed a long way off and he didn't appreciate the need to plan a path that would take him there. Somehow he managed to fly under the radar, with no particular adult paying special attention to what he was doing at school. Without older brothers or sisters with university experience, he didn't have anyone who could advise him at a time when he was making his choices.

The first year of NCEA in Year 11 was not too bad. Jason had to take maths, science and English, and he chose computing and metalwork as his other subjects.

YEAR 11 NCEA SUBJECTS	COMMENTS
Level 1 English	Compulsory at this level. It is important to achieve literacy credits for NCEA Level 1, and to meet the prerequisites for more advanced study in English and related subjects at Level 2.
Level 1 Mathematics	Compulsory at this level. It is important to achieve numeracy credits for NCEA Level 1, and to meet the prerequisites for more advanced study in maths and related subjects at Level 2.
Level 1 Science	Compulsory at this level (at Jason's school). This is an important prerequisite for later studies in chemistry, physics or biology.
Level 1 Computer technology	Optional subject. It appealed to Jason because it would allow him to "play with computers" and surf the web.
Level 1 Materials technology (metalwork)	Optional subject. Jason chose it because he liked the practical skills he thought he would develop, and because his best friend was doing it.

Year 12 was the critical year for Jason. With good advice he might have been able to keep his options open. Instead, and even though he had achieved NCEA Level 1 with over 90 credits, he decided to take two further Level 1 subjects—in accounting and hospitality. He thought that accounting might be interesting and that completing some credits in hospitality would help him get after-school work at the local café. Computer technology did not fit into his timetable so he chose sport and recreation instead. His Year 12 subjects were as follows.

YEAR 12 NCEA SUBJECTS	COMMENTS
Level 2 English	Compulsory at this level. It is important to achieve literacy credits for UE, and for the continuing development of critical thinking, writing and presentation skills.
Level 2 Mathematics	Compulsory at this level. Maths with algebra is also essential preparation for more advanced study of statistics and calculus.
Level 2 Sport & recreation	Optional subject. Outdoor activities appealed to Jason, so he did not mind taking this subject, although the main reason was that it fitted his timetable.
Level 1 Accounting	Optional subject. Given his overall interests and possible future studies in computer engineering or information technology, this was not a good choice.
Level 1 Hospitality	Optional subject. As for Level 1 accounting, this also was not the best choice for Jason. He did not need additional Level 1 credits, and his plans for the future did not include anything to do with hospitality.

Jason worked hard, and even though he did only three Level 2 subjects he achieved enough credits to complete NCEA Level 2. The problem was that by the end of Year 12 he had added another 35 Level 1 credits to his record, which he did not need and which did little to prepare him for tertiary study.

At the start of Year 13 Jason decided that he wanted to go to university the following year, with the hope of getting into a computer engineering programme. His Year 12 record made it difficult to get into the Level 3 classes he needed to do. He was fine with English, but did not have enough appropriate Level 2 credits in maths to get into Level 3 calculus, or to take physics—two subjects that are really important for anyone wanting to do engineering. After his form teacher intervened, he was allowed to enrol in Level 3 physical education and social studies. At least these subjects were on the approved list for UE. His study programme was as follows.

YEAR 13 NCEA SUBJECTS	COMMENTS
Level 3 English	English is important for the continuing development of critical thinking, writing and presentation skills. It also helped to keep Jason's options open for future study.
Level 3 Statistics	This is a relevant option for students going on to study sciences or engineering, although calculus might be preferred for some degrees.
Level 3 Social studies	This is helpful in terms of general education and its contribution toward UE, but physics would have been a better option for study in science or engineering.
Level 3 Physical education	This is helpful in terms of general education and its contribution toward UE, but of little direct relevance for computer engineering.

During the year Jason became aware of the poor preparation he had for the subjects he was trying to study in Year 13, but there was nothing he could do about it. He found it particularly difficult to keep motivated in the social studies class and did not sit the external exam at the end of the year.

JASON'S EXPERIENCE IS NOT UNCOMMON

By the end of Year 13 Jason had completed only 44 Level 3 credits in total—not enough for the Level 3 Certificate or to give him admission to degree-level studies at university. In terms of his hopes of studying computer engineering, he lacked one essential subject (physics), his preparation in mathematics was less than ideal, and he didn't have enough credits (or the grades) to compete for a place in the university programme of his choice.

If he still wanted to pursue his dream of studying computer engineering, Jason would need to go back to school to complete additional subjects, or complete a bridging programme in a university or polytechnic, and then try again.

Jason's experience is not uncommon. He was a student with no definite goals to work towards, and was therefore not clear about what path to take through the NCEA years. He lacked adult mentors, with his parents unaware that he could have made different subject choices or that they could have been more active in helping him map a path towards university education. Somehow, he also missed getting timely academic advice at school, so it was difficult to make up for the poor choices made in previous years. Academic ability—which Jason had in abundance—was not enough. Good planning, understanding the implications of different subject choices and having access to sound academic advice or counselling are just as important.

KEY POINTS

It's easy to be wise when looking back. Making the right choices and staying on a solid educational path from year to year is a bit more challenging. So what lessons are there in these three stories for students yet to embark on their NCEA journeys?

- If you are interested in science, or any job or career with a significant science component, make sure you seek good advice, plan early and stay on track in terms of the subjects you will need to do during your high school years.

- Make sure you take the right versions of core subjects, such as maths and sciences, that not only include externally assessed standards but are also regarded as prerequisites for more advanced study in subsequent years. And make sure you complete enough credits to meet the subject pass or prerequisite rules your school will have for progression to higher-level study in particular subjects.

- Maths, and science subjects such as chemistry or physics require a solid understanding of basic principles and laws, and are difficult to pick up at a more advanced level when this basic understanding is lacking. So an early start is essential.

- Talk with your science teachers or the Head of Science at your school. Make them aware of your interests and plans and ask them to help you plan your studies to ensure that, if you still wish, you will be able to complete the Level 3 maths and science subjects expected of students wanting to go on to study science-based courses at university.

- Remember that other subjects are also important, and that you might be wise to keep your options open, so studying languages, history, geography, drama, music or sports-related subjects can broaden your perspectives, develop your critical thinking, writing and creative skills, and open other career options.

- There are people in all schools—such as deans, career guidance teachers, form teachers and student counsellors—who can help you make good decisions.

- And if at the end of it all you change your mind and move away from science, or even from going to university, your learning will not be wasted. You will draw on the knowledge you have acquired and find ways to put it to good use.

3
IF YOU PREFER ARTS AND SOCIAL SCIENCES

INTRODUCTION

Maybe your interests and future career plans lie in becoming a:
- teacher of history, languages, music, arts or social sciences
- lawyer
- sociologist
- museum curator
- journalist
- counsellor or social worker
- clinical or organisational psychologist
- philosopher
- specialist in media and communication
- film maker, producer or editor
- performer in music, drama or dance
- politician (or political analyst)
- diplomat.

There are many options for study and careers that require broad general knowledge, creativity, analytical and critical thinking skills, and strong verbal and written communication skills. Just as it is important to plan your studies if your interests lie in science (see Chapter 2), so it is important to plan what subjects to take and how to organise your NCEA studies if your interests are in the general areas of arts, humanities or social sciences. The three stories in this chapter show how different students might plan—or fail to plan—their pathway through NCEA.

JESSICA

Sitting in a classroom, Jessica might appear quiet and shy, but she actually loves performing in front of a crowd. She loves singing, playing the guitar and taking part in school plays and cultural group performances. In Year 9 she started to play the saxophone and is now in the school band. Her teachers think she has real talent for music and acting. Jessica's older brother got into trouble at school and left at the end of Year 12 without any qualifications, but her parents are keen for Jessica to stay at school through to Year 13 and maybe go on to university to become a teacher.

JESSICA IS NOT YET SURE WHAT SHE WANTS TO DO AFTER SCHOOL

At the start of Year 11 Jessica is not yet sure what she wants to do after school, but she is keen to study the subjects she enjoys and learn as much as she can. Jessica is especially keen to take optional subjects that include opportunities to be part of a group and perform on stage.

Because she attends a school where all students have to take six subjects in the first 2 years of NCEA, and do English, maths and physical education in Year 11, Jessica's Year 11 subjects are as follows.

YEAR 11 NCEA SUBJECTS	COMMENTS
Level 1 English	Compulsory at this level. It is important to achieve literacy credits for NCEA Level 1, and to meet the prerequisites for more advanced study in English and related subjects at Level 2.
Level 1 Mathematics	Compulsory at this level. It is important to achieve numeracy credits for NCEA Level 1, and to meet the prerequisites for more advanced study in maths and related subjects at Level 2.
Level 1 Physical education & health	Compulsory at this level (at Jessica's school). Physical education encourages students to adopt healthy lifestyles and be physically active.

Level 1 Music	Optional subject. Jessica's focus was on guitar and saxophone as solo instruments, and on performing in the school band to add the experience of performing in a group.
Level 1 Māori performing arts	Optional subject. This is important to Jessica in terms of her ethnic identity and creative expression. The subject focuses on Māori dance forms and allowed her to take part in the regional kapa haka competition as part of the school group.
Level 1 Drama	Optional subject. Drama appealed to Jessica's creative side and provided the possibility of being selected for the school play.

In Year 12 Jessica had to take English and maths, and four other subjects. She decided to leave physical education and pick up history. Having done well in all her subjects, but especially in drama and Māori performing arts, Jessica was encouraged to add some Level 3 standards to these subjects. Her Year 12 programme was as follows.

YEAR 12 NCEA SUBJECTS	COMMENTS
Level 2 English	Compulsory at this level. It is important to achieve literacy credits for UE, and for the continuing development of critical thinking, writing and presentation skills.
Level 2 Mathematics	Compulsory at this level. It is important to achieve numeracy credits for NCEA Level 1, and to meet the prerequisites for more advanced study in maths and related subjects at Level 2.
Level 2 History	Optional subject. The subject appealed to Jessica because of the content, but also because it would allow her to continue with history at Level 3 or do classical studies instead.
Level 2 Music	Optional subject. Jessica's focus continued on guitar and saxophone as solo instruments, along with performing in the school band.

Levels 2 & 3 Māori performing arts	Optional subject. This subject focused on poi and waiata. If her school group qualified, and her parents agreed, she would be able to take part in national kapa haka competition.
Levels 2 & 3 Drama	Optional subject. She was able to focus on drama production and script writing, and auditioned for one of the lead roles in the school play.

In her final year at school Jessica needed to take five subjects. There were no compulsory subjects any more, but her parents had encouraged her to focus on the subjects that would give her the best possible preparation for university study. At this stage she decided to aim for an arts degree.

Jessica showed herself to be a very talented and hard-working student and was encouraged by her teachers to consider sitting Scholarship exams in at least two subjects—English and drama. Winning a Scholarship award would be a great achievement, boosting Jessica's confidence and helping pay for some of the costs of university study. But it also meant extra work and aiming for Merits and Excellences. Jessica's Year 13 subjects were as follows.

YEAR 13 NCEA SUBJECTS	COMMENTS
Level 3 English	English is important for the continuing development of critical thinking, writing and presentation skills. Jessica excelled in this subject in Year 12 and enjoyed her studies.
Level 3 History	She enjoyed history in Year 12 and found it helpful in developing her research and independent study skills.
Level 3 Classical studies	With a background in history and English, Jessica was able to choose this subject. She hoped that she would be able to read about classical Greece, and especially Greek theatre.

Level 3 Drama	Jessica excelled in drama in Year 12. She hoped to be able to focus on drama production and writing in her studies, and to gain experience as the assistant director for the school musical.
Level 3 Music	She picked up percussion as an additional solo discipline and joined the new jazz ensemble started by a new music teacher.

Jessica made a number of important decisions at the beginning of her final year of high school. She decided not to take Māori performing arts as a subject for Level 3 NCEA, in part because she had already achieved some Level 3 credits in the subject, but also because she wanted to focus on the approved subjects and achieving as many credits as possible with Merit and Excellence. With her increasing focus on arts subjects, she also decided to drop maths and do more history. She was selected to be the head prefect and wanted to put a lot of energy into the school musical. All that, plus the prospect of Scholarship exams, was going to be quite a challenge.

At the end of her secondary schooling Jessica had done very well and was ready to move on to university study. She was excited at the prospect of studying drama and music education within a Bachelor of Arts degree. She hoped her studies would eventually take her into stage and film work. Had she wanted to change her plans, she would have been just as well prepared to study history or English literature, primary or secondary school teaching, or an area of social sciences such as anthropology, philosophy or sociology.

BENJI

Benji is a bit of an enigma to his teachers. Sometimes you might think that all he is interested in is playing sport. He loves team sports: rugby, league, touch football, even basketball. You can see his leadership coming through in the way he talks to other guys during a game and motivates them to try harder. But there is more to Benji than his love of sport.

Benji's family is part of a church that is very active in its community, especially with young people. There is a homework centre after school, a youth choir, a cultural group, and a youth club on Friday nights. His dad has even organised weekend tramping trips and a youth camp, trying to keep some of the young people from getting into trouble with alcohol and gangs.

Benji's aim is to work with young people—in community development or counselling, or using sport to help troubled teenagers stay out of serious trouble. His parents think he should become a teacher so he can have a secure job, but Benji is not ready to decide just yet.

At his school, students have to take five subjects each year, and English, maths and science are compulsory in Year 11. So his Level 1 NCEA subject choices were as follows.

YEAR 11 NCEA SUBJECTS	COMMENTS
Level 1 English	Compulsory at this level. It is important to achieve literacy credits for NCEA Level 1, and to meet the prerequisites for more advanced study in English and related subjects at Level 2.
Level 1 Mathematics	Compulsory at this level. It is important to achieve numeracy credits for NCEA Level 1, and to meet the prerequisites for more advanced study in maths and related subjects at Level 2.
Level 1 Science	Compulsory at this level (at Benji's school). This is an important prerequisite for later studies in chemistry, physics or biology, although Benji is not so keen on physics.
Level 1 Physical education	Optional subject. However, this is Benji's favourite and he looks forward to playing rugby and touch.

Level 1 Geography	Optional subject. Benji likes the prospect of learning about different countries and parts of the world, and the idea of a field trip to Mt Tongariro in the spring sounds awesome.

Having done well in Year 11 (a total of 105 credits and the Level 1 certificate with Merit), Benji was ready to move to Level 2 NCEA. He had to do English and either maths or a science subject in Year 12, but could choose the other three subjects. Both his form teacher and his parents encouraged him to keep his options open and continue with academic subjects as well as following his passion for sport. He trialled for the school's First XV rugby team and was made a prefect at school, as well as a youth group leader at his church. Balancing all these commitments would be really important. His subject choices were as follows.

YEAR 12 NCEA SUBJECTS	COMMENTS
Level 2 English	Compulsory at this level. It is important to achieve literacy credits for UE, and for the continuing development of critical thinking, writing and presentation skills.
Level 2 Mathematics	Compulsory at this level. It is important to achieve numeracy credits for NCEA Level 1, and to meet the prerequisites for more advanced study in maths and related subjects at Level 2. This was not Benji's first choice, but he took the advice to complete at least 16 credits so that he could, if he wanted, do Level 3 maths the following year.
Level 2 Physical education	Optional subject. This is still Benji's favourite subject. He was selected to play in the First XV team as well as touch and basketball.
Level 2 Health	Optional subject. The content appealed to Benji, especially adolescent and mental health issues. It fits his timetable better than biology, which was his alternative subject.

Level 2 Social studies	Optional subject. Topics such as values, society and social action interest him, and Benji is also looking forward to choosing a topic for independent study.

Benji not only excelled in sport in Year 12 but also attained NCEA Level 2 (achieving Excellence endorsements in health and physical education, and Merit endorsements in English and social studies). His interest in youth work had deepened and he narrowed his choices to social work or physical education. (Psychology looked attractive, but Benji was afraid that it would take him away from his passion for sport and working with young people.)

BENJI'S AIM IS TO WORK WITH YOUNG PEOPLE

During his final year at school he sought out more detailed information about these options. To help him make the final decision he was able to visit two universities that offer social work and physical education degrees. With a bit of guidance and encouragement from his basketball coach towards the end of the year, he applied for scholarships from several community and philanthropic organisations. Each might be only $500 or $1,000, but the money would certainly help get him started at university. Benji's Year 13 programme was as follows.

YEAR 13 NCEA SUBJECTS	COMMENTS
Level 3 English	English is important for continuing the development of critical thinking, writing and presentation skills—it's not all about sport.
Level 3 Statistics	Even though this was not his top choice last year, he enjoyed the academic challenge. Statistics could be very important depending on which degree he decides on.

Level 3 Social studies	Benji needed to do at least four approved subjects and he had the necessary prerequisites for this one. In any case, Benji was interested in social issues and trying to work out where he stands and how his values and beliefs influence his views.
Level 3 Physical education	This is still Benji's favourite subject, so it helped that it was on the approved list.
Level 3 Sports Academy	He was invited to join the Sports Academy as one of the best athletes at the school. Sports Academy does not count towards UE or in ranking scores for entry to university, so Benji needed to do extremely well in his other subjects to get the credits that would help him get into university. Benji was appointed captain of the First XV team and played for the regional rugby club (junior team). He also trained to cycle in the Lake Taupo Cycle Challenge with members of his youth club.

Taking Sports Academy was a bit of a gamble because this subject does not count towards UE or in ranking scores for entry to university. It is assessed for NCEA but is made up of a mix of Level 1 to Level 3 unit standards. It also requires serious commitment in terms of fitness and participation in sport. On the other hand, it did give Benji the opportunity to develop his leadership and public speaking skills, and to test his sports skills. It could be a step up to a professional rugby career, but Benji was sure that as much as he enjoyed sport, preparation for university study was still his priority.

So which path did Benji choose at the end of his final year at school? He loved being the rugby team captain and playing for the regional rugby club. Sport remains his passion. He hopes to be able to play for the university rugby team, and maybe even captain it. But his priorities have firmed up and he is applying for admission to a 4-year degree in physical education. He considered applying for a degree in social work or human services (with a major in youth services practice), and was well prepared for it, but teaching health and physical education to secondary school students and staying active in sport finally tipped the scales in favour of physical education.

The only catch, as far as Benji can see, is that instead of the more typical 3 years, this degree will take 4 years. The costs of an extra year will be a challenge for his family, especially as his younger brother will be ready for tertiary study in 2 years' time. So Benji is following up on any opportunities he can find for summer work—pity all those summer camps in the USA take place during New Zealand winter! Strawberry picking might have to do for now. And he is hoping that of the five applications for scholarships he sent off recently, at least a couple will come through.

LUCY

Like Jessica and Benji, Lucy is interested in people and ideas more than maths or science. She is a bit of a chatter-box, talking, texting and spending every free moment on Facebook. If she is ever in trouble at school it's because she is always talking in class—she just can't help it. That can be a bit of a problem, because she knows that some of her teachers think she is not all that interested in her studies, or that she will never be able to cope with serious subjects like chemistry. Well, maybe.

LUCY IS QUITE HAPPY TO GO WITH THE FLOW

Lucy is quite happy to go with the flow. She likes being in the same classes as her best friends and has changed her mind umpteen times about what she wants to be when she leaves school—air hostess, beautician, tourist guide, or maybe a lawyer. She likes arguing; not in a mean way, but just to see if she can win the point. Her mum thinks she should join a debating team or a speech competition at school to channel all that talk to some good use!

When she started Year 11 Lucy was not sure if she wanted to go to university. Except that her dad thought that she was the smartest one in the family and could one day be a member of parliament or a university professor. Lucy's dad is great: always the optimist. But when it comes to Lucy's future he is not the only one. Lucy's aunty Aroha, who sits on the City Council and the Board of Trustees of her children's school, and works as a social worker at the local hospital, is a bit of a talker herself. She has said many times that Lucy has real potential! All she needs is a bit of focus and application; decide what she wants to achieve and go for it. It might take a bit of hard work, but hard work never did her any harm, and Lucy could do with some hard work. Trouble is that Lucy has done OK at school so far, relying on her natural talents, and not having to work as hard as some of her friends to get a passing grade.

At this stage Lucy was not too worried what she might study later on. She was quite happy with her Year 11 choices. English, maths and science were compulsory at this level, so no point in arguing about that. For her three optional subjects she chose health, fashion & design, and French. So here is her Year 11 programme.

YEAR 11 NCEA SUBJECTS	COMMENTS
Level 1 English	Compulsory at this level. It is important to achieve literacy credits for NCEA Level 1, and to meet the prerequisites for more advanced study in English and related subjects at Level 2.
Level 1 Mathematics	Compulsory at this level. It is important to achieve numeracy credits for NCEA Level 1, and to meet the prerequisites for more advanced study in maths and related subjects at Level 2.

Level 1 Science	Compulsory at this level (at Lucy's school). This is an important prerequisite for later studies in chemistry, physics or biology.
Level 1 Health	Optional subject. Lucy expected it would be interesting. It was either health or physical education on the timetable, and physical exertion is not Lucy's thing.
Level 1 French	Optional subject. Lucy took French in Year 10 and did quite well, so she had the necessary prerequisite. She also liked the fact that she would have the same teacher as in Year 10.
Level 1 Fashion & design	Optional subject. Lucy expected this to be a fun subject and an easy way to get lots of credits. It would suit her creative talents (and her best friend was taking it too).

Lucy's Year 11 results were a bit of a mixed bag. She achieved the Level 1 certificate, but missed out on getting the necessary numeracy credits for a subject pass to continue with the academic version of maths the following year. Lucy did not think that was a great loss, but it did narrow her Level 2 choices. French turned out to be harder than Lucy expected, so she was not sure that she wanted to continue with it, even though the trip to a French restaurant (speaking only French) was great fun. Lucy also enjoyed the work she did in fashion and design class, with lots of opportunities to show her creative talents and flair for colours. But unless she wanted to go on in this field, taking fashion & design at Levels 2 and 3 might not be her best choice. It is not an approved subject for UE, and with unit standards only it did not offer her the opportunity to achieve with Merit or Excellence, which Lucy was starting to think might be quite important. Going with the flow was proving to be a bit of a headache.

So here was her programme for Year 12.

YEAR 12 NCEA SUBJECTS	COMMENTS
Level 2 English	Compulsory at this level. It is important to achieve literacy credits for UE, and for the continuing development of critical thinking, writing and presentation skills.
Level 2 Mathematics	Compulsory at this level. It is important to achieve numeracy credits for NCEA Level 1, and to meet the prerequisites for more advanced study in maths and related subjects at Level 2. Having failed to achieve enough credits for a subject pass at Level 1, Lucy was placed in a practical maths class.
Level 2 Biology	Optional subject. Lucy would have preferred health, but it clashed with her other choices. She hoped the subject would not have too much science in it.
Level 2 Fashion & design	This was an optional subject but one that Lucy enjoyed. It helped that it fitted into her timetable and her friends were also continuing with it.
Level 2 Media studies	Optional subject. She hoped this subject would help her learn what is involved in working in the public media.
Level 1 Economics	Optional subject. Lucy was able to use the flexibility of NCEA to study at Level 1. She had considered the possibility of business studies at university, so Level 1 economics could prove helpful.

Lucy ended her Year 12 with results that fell well short of her potential. Halfway through the year she lost interest in maths and did not submit all the assignments for internal assessments. She did quite well in biology but having got her 14 credits from internal assessments did not turn up for the external exam. Economics was OK too, but not a subject that excited her.

You would think that Lucy might be a bit of a lost cause—swapping and changing all the time and not at all sure where she wants to go. But she did really well in English and media studies, and she won a prize for the T-shirts she designed in her fashion and design class. The big question was, what was she going to do next year? Some of her friends were thinking of not coming back to school, especially if they could find jobs, but her parents were having none of that. Lucy was going back, whether she felt like it or not. So here were her Year 13 subjects.

YEAR 13 NCEA SUBJECTS	COMMENTS
Level 3 English	English is important for the continuing development of critical thinking, writing and presentation skills. Lucy had done well in this subject in Year 12 and enjoyed her studies.
Level 3 Media studies	Lucy enjoyed this subject in Year 12 and did well in it. It is on the approved list for UE.
Level 3 Biology	She had done enough in this subject in Year 12 to be allowed to take it at this level.
Level 3 Social studies	This was one of the few approved subjects she was allowed to do without prior study and that also fitted into her timetable. (Lucy did not have the necessary prerequisites for maths or other science subjects, or for subjects such as history or geography, so this was a compromise option.)
Levels 2 and 3 French	She was able to take a combination of Level 2 and Level 3 standards. Looking back, dropping this subject in Year 12 was not the best decision, but a combined Level 2 and Level 3 class allowed her to pick up the subject again and achieve some Level 3 credits.

Lucy did a lot of growing up over the summer before her last year of high school. Working late nights at the local fast food outlet taught her the importance of turning up on time, working in a team, and how hard it is to earn money (and how easy to spend it). She enjoyed meeting the customers, especially the regulars: like the tradesmen (always in a rush), or the grandparents sharing a treat with their grandchildren, or the homeless man (carefully counting his coins and taking his time over the coffee with six sugars).

Even though she was far from clear what she wanted to do when she left school, Lucy decided that she had to make the most of her last year at school and give herself a chance to go on to university. Talking with the career guidance teacher helped her to consider options she had not thought about before: a Bachelor of Arts in sociology, or political studies, or anthropology; or a degree in communication and media; or in European studies and international relations.

So how did Lucy do? Well, not as well as she thought she would, but well enough to achieve UE, and the minimum number of points for entry to an Arts degree. So she is university bound, taking a mix of arts and social science courses in her first year and then deciding which direction to follow. So that's the plan, for now!

KEY POINTS

Just as in the case of students choosing the science pathway, so students aiming for university study in the arts and social sciences need to plan their NCEA course choices with care. Jessica's and Benji's stories show that having a passion for drama, music, or sports is a great motivator, but the passion has to be combined with solid academic study, good information, planning, and decisions that involve the mind as well as the heart.

Lucy's story, on the other hand, shows what can happen to students who are happy to go with the flow and not consider the consequences of their choices until it might be almost too late. It would have been helpful if Lucy's school had a system of tracking their students' progress and providing timely academic advice to students and their parents. Lucy's parents recognised her potential and had great aspirations and hopes for their daughter. The problem was that they did not have the information or the strategies to help her achieve her full potential at school.

So the points to remember.

- There are many options for university study and careers in the broad area of arts, humanities and social sciences, but planning the NCEA pathway and choosing the most appropriate courses at school is still very important.

- Literacy skills are essential, not just in terms of knowing how to structure a sentence or use punctuation: curiosity, critical thinking and the ability to express yourself verbally and in writing are just as important. It is important to choose NCEA subjects that will help you develop these skills and challenge you to think deeply and logically.

- There are no right or wrong subjects individually, but deciding which subjects will create the best possible path towards a goal is important from the start.

- The more specialised the university degree you plan to achieve (music, visual or performing arts, art and design, languages), the more important it is to take these subjects early, and to take them right through the senior years of high school.

- Make sure you take the right versions of core subjects such as English. If English is not your first language and you need additional help, make sure that your school is aware of the amount and kind of help you need. Needing help to improve your fluency in English doesn't mean that you can't catch up and achieve at the more advanced levels in English and in other subjects (such as history, media studies or economics) that require strong literacy skills.

- Achieving subject passes at each level is important so that you can progress to more advanced levels of study. This relates not only to the total number of credits, but can often mean achievement in specific standards. Make sure you know what these are at the beginning of each year.

- Keeping your options open is still important, even if you are sure that the only thing you want to study at university is drama, or politics, or any other subject. Plan for what you want to do, but do it in a way that keeps other doors open.

- Good numeracy skills are important too, especially for social sciences such as sociology, geography or economics, which rely on statistics in their research. So achieving at least Level 2 maths and having some grounding in statistics could be quite important.

- Work on developing independent study skills because you will need them as soon as you get to university. Science subjects tend to be more structured, with regular laboratory sessions and structured manuals to follow. In arts and social sciences much of your learning will depend on independent reading, researching self-selected assignment topics, and being able to play with ideas and use reasoning and logic to demonstrate what you have learned.

- More than any other area of study, arts and social sciences are likely to expose you to new subject areas that you had not considered before—philosophy, anthropology, political science, etc. Taking a range of subjects in the first year will give you a taste of what's available, so don't be afraid to change your mind if your original area of study is not what you expected, or you discover an exciting new subject and end up majoring in it.

4
IF BUSINESS AND COMMERCE IS WHERE YOU WANT TO BE

INTRODUCTION

For students looking to work in the area of business, management, finance or economics, there are many career opportunities, including:

- accounting
- business management
- financial planning
- human resource management
- public relations
- advertising and marketing
- market research
- taxation
- property development, management or valuation
- international trade
- commercial law
- economics
- business information systems.

Some students might be interested in business and commerce because they hope to start their own businesses, work in import or export areas, or develop a management career in the public sector (government departments, universities, health services), or with one of the large national or multinational firms. There are many different university degrees that can help prepare you for a career in business or management, and different universities offer similar degrees under different names, or degrees that sound the same but might be quite different. It pays to check carefully whether a degree in "business", "business studies" or "commerce" will allow you to major in the subject of most interest and relevance to you, whether this is finance, marketing, human resource management, or another field.

JACK

Jack decided quite early on that one day he would be working as an executive for a multinational company such as Saatchi & Saatchi, or PricewaterhouseCoopers. Even though neither of his parents attended university, both have worked hard and are self-employed running a small business. They have also insisted that Jack learn the value of hard work, so he has always had to earn his pocket money—doing dishes, making his own lunch, mowing lawns, and keeping the two family cars clean and polished (even before he was allowed to drive them). More recently, he has had a regular after-school job stacking supermarket shelves, and saving 20 percent of his pay for when he goes to university.

JACK WORKS HARD, DURING AND AFTER SCHOOL. HE ALSO PLAYS HARD.

Jack works hard, during and after school. He also plays hard. He loves surfing and the whole beach scene, working on his car, parties, loud music and drinking. He is about to enrol at university and take the next step towards his dream job. But how did he get to this point?

In Year 11 Jack took the compulsory subjects: English, maths and science, making sure these included the standards that would lead to more advanced study later. He also did his homework, and carefully checked what optional subjects he should take. At his school he was required to take six subjects. Because he was determined to complete a conjoint degree and knew that getting in would be very competitive, he was aware from the start of the need to demonstrate his academic abilities by achieving with Merit and Excellence. These were his Year 11 choices.

YEAR 11 NCEA SUBJECTS	COMMENTS
Level 1 English	Compulsory at this level. It is important to achieve literacy credits for NCEA Level 1, and to meet the prerequisites for more advanced study in English and related subjects at Level 2.
Level 1 Mathematics	Compulsory at this level. It is important to achieve numeracy credits for NCEA Level 1, and to meet the prerequisites for more advanced study in maths and related subjects at Level 2.
Level 1 Science	Compulsory at this level (at Jack's school). This is important if Jack wants to keep his options open and choose biology, chemistry or physics at Level 2.
Level 1 Economics	Optional subject. Economics is relevant to university study in business and commerce.
Level 1 Accounting	Optional subject. Accounting is relevant to university study in business and commerce.
Level 1 History	Optional subject. History is relevant in terms of general education and the development of critical thinking and writing skills.

Having done really well in Year 11 (achieving Level 1 Certificate, endorsed with Excellence), the challenge for Jack was to keep the momentum going, to study as hard and do as well in Year 12. He needed to continue with the core subjects of English and maths, and chose to continue with economics and accounting in order to remain on a clear track to a university degree in business. He also decided to continue with science, choosing biology, but had second thoughts about history and chose geography as his sixth subject.

YEAR 12 NCEA SUBJECTS	COMMENTS
Level 2 English	Compulsory at this level. English is important for achieving literacy credits for UE, and for the continuing development of critical thinking, writing and presentation skills.
Level 2 Mathematics	Compulsory at this level. Maths with algebra is also essential preparation for more advanced study of statistics and calculus.
Level 2 Biology	A science subject is required at Jack's school at this level.
Level 2 Economics	Optional subject. Economics is relevant to university study in business and commerce.
Level 2 Accounting	Optional subject. Accounting is relevant to university study in business and commerce.
Level 2 Geography	Optional subject. Geography is relevant in terms of general education and the development of critical thinking and writing skills. (Jack needed special approval to do Level 2 geography because he had not done it at Level 1, but his overall performance at Level 1 was enough to convince the head of geography to let him do it.)

By the end of Year 12 Jack had built a strong academic record and could easily have opted to specialise in either science or business in his final year at school. Reviewing his accomplishments to this point, and the options open to him, Jack decided to stay with his original plan, aiming for a conjoint degree in law and economics. One of his teachers also encouraged him to become involved in YES (the Young Enterprise Scheme), administered by the Young Enterprise Trust and offered through some schools. It involves a team of students starting a business and acting as its board of directors in order to design, market and sell a product. YES students are mentored by local business people, and assessed through internal assessment and final examination.

Because Jack is not active in group activities such as team sports, drama or cultural clubs, this would also be an opportunity to develop and test his skills in leadership and teamwork, interpersonal relations, and the business-related skills of budgeting, planning and risk management. What really appealed to Jack was the prospect of mentorship by successful business people from his community and being able to tap into their expertise. YES is not an NCEA subject (although it can be cross-credited towards an NCEA Certificate), and Jack decided to take it in addition to the five NCEA subjects rather than instead of one of them. His Year 13 programme was as follows.

YEAR 13 NCEA SUBJECTS	COMMENTS
Level 3 English	English is very relevant to study in law. It is also important for the continuing development of critical thinking, writing and presentation skills.
Level 3 Statistics	The university-level study of economics (especially econometrics) requires a solid grounding in maths. Research in economics also requires knowledge of statistics.
Level 3 Economics	Economics is relevant to university study in business and commerce.
Level 3 Accounting	Accounting is relevant to university study in business and commerce.
Level 3 Geography	Optional subject. Geography is relevant in terms of general education as well as to university study in business and commerce.
Non-NCEA subject Young Enterprise Scheme (YES)	Additional to the five approved subjects. YES provided Jack with the opportunity to test himself in a different context, test some of his ideas, and work in a team on a practical business project.

Jack was very focused in his NCEA studies. He knew where he wanted to go and he took the most obvious path to get there. (Doing economics and accounting at Level 3 was not essential: solid passes in English, mathematics, and history or classics might have done just as well in terms of getting into the programme. Nevertheless, Jack preferred getting an early start in these subjects and becoming familiar with all the words and ideas that are specific to them.)

The YES experience was valuable, although he almost made the mistake of putting so much effort into the project that his other subjects suffered. Almost, but not quite! It was a good lesson in time management and sticking to his priorities.

Having decided that he wanted to enrol for a conjoint degree, Jack checked the specific entry requirements at the university he wanted to attend. He worked out that if he did not achieve at least some credits with Merit or Excellence he would need over 100 Level 3 credits in five approved subjects. His choice was to aim for 16 to 18 credits in each of the five subjects, with at least half of all credits with Merit or higher.

Some university programmes require students to have completed specific subjects at Level 3 (e.g., chemistry for medicine, or physics for engineering), and Jack made sure that he also checked this requirement. He knew that all five approved subjects he did in Year 13 were on the list for the conjoint degree in commerce and law, so he would have no difficulty meeting that particular requirement.

The points systems used by different universities to rank students for entry to specific degree programmes might differ, but are usually based on 2 points for a credit at Achievement level, 3 points for a credit achieved with Merit and 4 points for a credit achieved with Excellence. The example below is based on the system used at the University of Auckland for the 2014 student intake. The overall score is calculated on the basis of:

- a maximum of five Level 3 subjects from the approved list
- a maximum of 24 credits from each subject (achievement standards only)
- 80 "best" credits.

To be assured of a place in the conjoint commerce and law (BCom/LLB) degree, Jack needed a rank score of 210. So how did Jack fare?

Table 2: Example of how a rank score for NCEA Level 3 is calculated

SUBJECT	RESULTS	CALCULATION	POINTS TOWARDS THE RANK SCORE
English	6 Excellence 6 Merit 14 Achieved	6 x 4 = 24 6 x 3 = 18 12 x 2 = 24*	66
Statistics	10 Merit 10 Achieved	10 x 3 = 30 10 x 2 = 20	50
Economics	4 Excellence 4 Merit 12 Achieved	4 x 4 = 16 4 x 3 = 12 12 x 2 = 24	52
Accounting	16 Merit 10 Achieved**	16 x 3 = 48	48
Geography	14 Achieved**		No score
YES	NCEA equivalent of 24 Achieved***		No score
Rank score			216

* A maximum of 24 credits per subject. Any credits above this limit are not counted.
** A maximum of 80 credits is used in calculating the rank score. Credits achieved with Excellence and Merit are counted first. Additional credits are excluded from the calculation.
*** Only subjects on the approved list count, and only five subjects can be included. Therefore, YES credits excluded from the calculation.

On the basis of his NCEA results, Jack achieved a rank score above the minimum of 210 points and would therefore be guaranteed a place in the conjoint degree of his choice. But take a closer look at what he had to achieve to get there. He completed five Level 3 subjects on the approved list and a total of 106 Level 3 credits, 46 of them with Merit or Excellence, plus the 24 credits from the Young Enterprise Scheme. This is a lot more than the minimum requirement for UE.

Had Jack failed to achieve the required rank score for the conjoint degree he might still have got in, but this would have depended on how many other students applied and how many ranked above him. If he did not gain entry to a conjoint degree he could have enrolled in the Bachelor of Commerce or the Bachelor of Business & Information Management as single degrees (with the required rank score of 180), or a Bachelor of Arts (with a required rank score of 150). Any of these options would have allowed him to include first-year law papers, and if he achieved at least a B+ average in law and other papers he would have qualified for selection into second-year law (an LLB degree).

(To put Jack's achievement in perspective, UE with three NCEA Level 3 subjects on the approved list with 20 credits in each, none above Achieved, would have gained a rank score of 120. Not enough to be assured of a place for any undergraduate degree at the University of Auckland, but possibly enough points for enrolment at another university.)

At the end of Year 13, Jack learned another lesson. A party to celebrate the end of NCEA exams he helped organise got out of hand. Beer bottles were thrown into the neighbour's garden smashing against a fence post, a couple of his friends were injured in a fight, and police were called in. It was a close call. Getting a police record was hardly the way Jack wanted to start his brilliant career.

ANNA

Anna comes from a family of six children. She has an older brother who is training to be a policeman, so she is the oldest one at home. That means looking after her younger brothers and sisters, making sure they have breakfast and are ready for school in the mornings, refereeing their squabbles, helping with dinner, and tidying up all the time. Anna's parents work long hours so she knows they depend on her to look after the younger ones. Sometimes she resents all the responsibility heaped on her, but mostly she just gets on with what needs to be done. Talk about learning to manage people! Anna is an expert in gentle but firm persuasion.

Seeing how hard her parents have to work—her mum for the minimum hourly rate—Anna is determined to get a professional qualification and have a career that will give her independence and financial security. She will be the first in her family to go to university. That's both scary and exciting. What drives Anna is her dream of one day running her own business, and taking her mum on a Pacific cruise. Just the two of them, with no meals to prepare and no dishes to do! She also knows that her parents expect her to set an example for her younger brothers and sisters. If she can succeed, then maybe they will follow.

LOOKING AFTER PEOPLE MIGHT BE MORE INTERESTING THAN DEALING WITH NUMBERS ALL DAY

Anna likes numbers and is a stickler for detail. She is good at budgeting the little bit of pocket money she gets from her parents, and the birthday and Christmas money gifts she gets from her grandmother. She likes the idea of being an accountant—looking after all the financial dealings of a company or business, keeping financial records, preparing financial reports, and analysing financial performance to identify how profitable the activities of the company are. Working for someone else at the beginning would be OK, but owning her own accountancy business one day would be even better. Even though accounting appeals to her, Anna is not sure that she should narrow her options just yet. Perhaps taking accounting as an NCEA subject will give her a better sense of what accountancy is all about and how well it might suit her.

Anna also likes the idea of working in human resource management, looking after people that work for a large organisation such as the city council or Air New Zealand—their recruitment, employment contracts, performance, benefits, health and safety, and professional development. She believes that all people should be treated with respect and that employers should understand that workers like her parents need support when they have a sick child or are unable to do overtime at short notice. Looking after people might be more interesting than dealing with numbers all day.

Given such different possibilities for a future career, Anna took the advice to keep her options open and chose her NCEA subjects with care. Her Year 11 programme reflected this.

YEAR 11 NCEA SUBJECTS	COMMENTS
Level 1 English	Compulsory at this level. It is important to achieve literacy credits for NCEA Level 1, and to meet the prerequisites for more advanced study in English and related subjects at Level 2.
Level 1 Mathematics	Compulsory at this level. It is important to achieve numeracy credits for NCEA Level 1, and to meet the prerequisites for more advanced study in maths and related subjects at Level 2.
Level 1 Science	Compulsory at this level (at Anna's school). Science is important if she wants to keep her options open and choose biology, chemistry or physics at Level 2.
Level 1 Accounting	Optional subject. Accounting is relevant to university study in business and commerce.
Level 1 Economics	Optional subject. Economics is relevant to university study in business and commerce.
Level 1 Geography	Optional subject. Geography is relevant in terms of general education and the development of critical thinking and writing skills.

During Year 11 Anna also played netball for the school junior team and joined the school choir. Although she was not intending to study music or physical education, she enjoyed singing and netball, and these activities gave her a chance to get away from books and study. It was her chance to be part of a group and to share in something they all enjoyed.

For Year 12 Anna chose to continue with English, mathematics, accounting, economics and geography, but decided to move away from science and take drama. She would have liked a subject like media studies or photography, to broaden her education, but these weren't available at her school. Even though she had not taken drama in Year 11, she had done well in English and received the Head of Department's approval to take Level 2 drama. So her six subjects in Year 12 were as follows.

YEAR 12 NCEA SUBJECTS	COMMENTS
Level 2 English	Compulsory at this level. It is important to achieve literacy credits for UE, and for the continuing development of critical thinking, writing and presentation skills.
Level 2 Mathematics	Compulsory at this level. Maths with algebra is also essential preparation for more advanced study of statistics and calculus.
Level 2 Accounting	Optional subject. Accounting is relevant to university study in business and commerce.
Level 2 Economics	Optional subject. Economics is relevant to university study in business and commerce.
Level 2 Geography	Optional subject. Geography is relevant in terms of general education and the development of critical thinking and writing skills.
Level 2 Drama	Optional subject. Drama is relevant in terms of general education and the development of creative and presentation skills.

Although she enjoyed all her subjects, especially mathematics, accounting and geography, Anna found Year 12 a lot more demanding than Year 11. The subjects she had chosen stretched her vocabulary, with new words and ideas introduced in almost every class. She had to be careful that she worked right through the year, did her homework and prepared well for all the assessments. Some of her friends seemed to be able to get away with little study, but she felt like she had to earn every credit.

Things at home did not help. Her mother had to have surgery during the year and was unable to work for 2 months, and that added to the stresses and strains at home. There was more housework for Anna to do, and less money coming in just when she needed new shoes for her geography field trip. It was also hard finding the time to study and do her homework. Still, netball gave her a chance to get rid of some of the frustrations, and whenever she could she used the school homework centre to get her work done.

Having excelled at Level 1, Anna did less well at Level 2. There were fewer Merits and Excellences and she even failed one standard in drama that she was hoping to scrape through. That was a huge disappointment. Still, she achieved the Level 2 Certificate and enough credits in each subject to be able to take the subjects she needed in Year 13.

It helped a lot that her form teacher reminded her that having got so far, what really mattered was how well she did in Year 13. So Anna approached Year 13 with determination to focus on doing her best academically. She decided to continue with netball, but as much as she enjoyed the choir, getting to all the practices was a challenge, and if something had to give, this would have to be it. Her five subjects for Year 13 were as follows.

YEAR 13 NCEA SUBJECTS	COMMENTS
Level 3 English	English is important for continuing the development of critical thinking, writing and presentation skills.
Level 3 Statistics	This is important for university studies in accounting and economics.
Level 3 Economics	Economics is relevant to university study in business and commerce.
Level 3 Accounting	Accounting is relevant to university study in business and commerce.
Level 3 Geography	It was a toss up between drama and geography. Anna chose geography because she felt she could achieve better grades, and that she would have better control of her time than in drama.

The focus, determination, and good time management paid off for Anna. She completed Year 13 with 96 Level 3 credits, all from approved subjects. She did particularly well in accounting and statistics and decided to apply for a degree in business with a major in accounting.

It isn't just that she is good with numbers. Anna also realised that she liked the sense of control she felt when dealing with mathematical problems, and that there was a definite job she would be qualified to do at the end of her university studies. It might not matter to other young people, but to Anna, feelings of security are important.

MICHAEL

Michael attended the same school as Anna. He comes from the same working-class community and knows that his parents expect him to "get an education". Just what that means is not entirely clear to Michael. He has no sense of what he wants to study at school or which way to go. He has lots of ideas though! He pictures himself running a big hotel somewhere, or being a famous TV chef, or designing trendy clothes with his own label. But there is also a practical side to Michael: he often cooks family meals when his mum works late, and he looks after his cousin's three young children when she works on the weekend.

> *HE PICTURES HIMSELF RUNNING A BIG HOTEL SOMEWHERE, OR BEING A FAMOUS TV CHEF, OR DESIGNING TRENDY CLOTHES WITH HIS OWN LABEL*

Michael is good at sports, a great dancer, a natural-born leader and (according to all the girls) good looking. And he is bright, too. He scored near the top of his class in mathematics and literacy tests in Year 10 and was placed in all the academic classes in Year 11. His teachers have high expectations for Michael. You would expect Michael to have an easy ride through NCEA. What could possibly go wrong?

Year 11 was not a problem, because Michael was placed in maths, science and English classes based on his Year 10 performance. He chose physical education, technology and hospitality as his optional subjects.

YEAR 11 NCEA SUBJECTS	COMMENTS
Level 1 English	Compulsory at this level. It is important to achieve literacy credits for NCEA Level 1, and to meet the prerequisites for more advanced study in English and related subjects at Level 2.
Level 1 Mathematics	Compulsory at this level. It is important to achieve numeracy credits for NCEA Level 1, and to meet the prerequisites for more advanced study in maths and related subjects at Level 2.
Level 1 Science	Compulsory at this level (at Michael's school). This is important if he wants to keep his options open and choose biology, chemistry or physics at Level 2.

Level 1 Physical education	Optional subject. This is not relevant to Michael's business or creative aspirations, but he chose it because he likes sport and likes being physically active.
Level 1 Technology (mechanical engineering)	Optional subject. This is also not particularly relevant to Michael's aspirations as his school does not offer graphics or fashion & design within the technology stream. He chose it because his friends were doing the subject and he wanted to learn how to fix cars.
Level 1 Hospitality	Optional subject. This is potentially relevant given Michael's interest in hotel management or becoming a chef, but it is made up of unit standards only and does not provide strong academic preparation for later study at university level.

Michael's choices in Year 11 reflected his varied interests and skills but were not particularly strategic. In other words, Michael chose subjects he had to do and subjects he thought would be interesting or enjoyable, rather than thinking how they might connect to specific subjects he would need to do later in order to prepare for university studies.

His Year 11 results were impressive. He achieved a total of 124 credits—26 of these in English, 28 in maths and 23 in science. Just as importantly, almost half of his credits in these subjects were with Merit or Excellence. A great start, and something to build on.

Then, somehow, Michael failed to receive good academic advice and his Year 12 choices took him off the path he needed to follow and into a mix of subjects and levels of study that reflected a lack of clear planning. He continued with English and mathematics and took biology as his science subject. He also continued with physical education (and was selected for the school's league team). At this point he decided that he wanted to study business at university and took Level 1 accounting and economics. So his Year 12 programme was as follows.

YEAR 12 NCEA SUBJECTS	COMMENTS
Level 2 English	Compulsory at this level. It is important to achieve literacy credits for UE, and for the continuing development of critical thinking, writing and presentation skills.
Level 2 Mathematics	Compulsory at this level. Maths with algebra is also essential preparation for more advanced study of statistics and calculus.
Level 1 Accounting	Optional subject. Accounting is relevant to university study in business and commerce, but Level 1 will not prepare Michael for Level 3 accounting the following year.
Level 1 Economics	Optional subject. Economics is relevant to university study in business and commerce, but Level 1 will not prepare Michael for Level 3 economics the following year.
Level 2 Biology	Optional subject. Biology is relevant in terms of general education and the development of writing skills.
Level 2 Physical education	Optional subject. This is Michael's favourite subject, because he has continued to excel at sports and did extremely well in the academic aspects as well.

You can see where Michael's passions were in Year 12. He achieved 27 credits in physical education but not enough credits in either economics or accounting to progress in these subjects the following year. He also achieved only 12 credits in mathematics, but did better in English and biology, achieving more credits, about a quarter of them with Merit or Excellence. His main problem was that he either did not turn up for the external exams (like mathematics) or walked out half-way through (in English and economics), feeling that he was not prepared enough to provide the answers he thought the examiners expected. The result was a total of 80 credits (enough to gain NCEA Level 2) and evidence that he could excel when he tried. But his record also showed a string of credits he failed to achieve—not because he was not able, but because he lacked confidence sitting external exams and did not appreciate how important this would be for his future options.

Given his study choices and achievements in Year 12, Michael was restricted in what subjects he could take in Year 13. He needed to take subjects approved for UE and he needed to do well enough to gain entry to a university programme that required more than the minimum UE standard. It was a lot to ask, but Michael wanted to give it a go. His teachers recognised what he needed to do but the school timetable made it difficult to be flexible in terms of the subjects he needed and that were available to him. His Year 13 programme was as follows.

YEAR 13 NCEA SUBJECTS	COMMENTS
Level 3 English	English is important for the continuing development of critical thinking, writing and presentation skills.
Level 3 Statistics	This is important for university studies in business and commerce.
Level 3 Biology	Approved subject for UE. Although not directly relevant to business (unless Michael chooses to study farm management or similar subjects), biology is important for the ongoing development of general education and writing skills.
Level 3 Physical education	Approved subject for UE. This is not directly relevant to business (unless Michael chooses to study sports management or similar subjects).
Non-NCEA subject Young Enterprise Scheme (YES)	This is not on the approved list for UE, but he is unable to take economics or accounting in Year 13, so Michael hopes to gain some business skills from the project.

For all his ability, Year 13 was a struggle for Michael. He had lost a lot of his earlier confidence, and found escape and reassurance on the sports field. He captained his league team to a series of victories in the inter-school competition, but found his academic studies a lot more challenging. Friends like Anna, who shared his English and maths classes, encouraged him to keep trying and to aim for university. The YES experience was not as helpful as he expected. The school YES team had difficulty getting regular mentoring from experienced business people, and the project that started as a good idea proved difficult to put into practice. It also took a lot of time—time that Michael needed to spend on his other subjects.

The NCEA results, when they came in January, were disappointing. Michael managed to achieve UE—but only just. He needed at least 16 credits in each of at least three subjects on the approved list for the degree in business and commerce. The list included English, statistics, and biology, but Michael had achieved fewer than 16 credits in all but statistics. He also needed a certain number of total points from the approved subjects, but with all credits at Achieved level and none with Merit or Excellence he fell short of that target as well.

Michael was advised to enrol in a Bridging Certificate programme that would prepare him for entry to a degree programme a year later. Such a programme could be a step-up, helping him to develop the knowledge and skills he would need to succeed at university, but it is a costly option. There are fees to be paid, and there is a delay in starting degree-level studies. For Michael this was a hard lesson to learn. Could he achieve a degree in business? Yes, he could. But if he had planned and been advised better from the beginning, like Jack and Anna, he could have gone straight into his degree studies well prepared and confident that he would succeed.

His other options included completing a Level 4 National Certificate in Business Administration, or a Level 6 National Certificate in Commerce through a polytechnic or other tertiary education providers. Neither is at a degree level, but either could be helpful as a starting point in a business career.

KEY POINTS

Students starting out on their NCEA journey might not think that their optional subjects in Year 11 matter a great deal, and often that is the case. But what Jack's, Anna's and Michael's stories show is that having a clear plan and selecting subjects carefully can make a huge difference. The NCEA system is flexible and will allow you to choose from a huge variety of subjects, but in the end you are limited to five or six in any one year, and in many areas you can only do more advanced subjects in Years 12 and 13 if you have done enough in that (or a related) subject at the previous level. So if you hope to study in the area of business and commerce, keep the following points in mind.

- Make sure you take mathematics *and* English (or history or classics) through to NCEA Level 3 and focus on the externally assessed (academic) versions of these subjects. Being able to express yourself clearly and confidently, both verbally and in writing, is very important.

- Economics and accounting can be very helpful, especially for students planning to major in these subjects, but they are not essential. If your interests lie in international trade, then geography, history or a language (Mandarin, Japanese, Spanish) could be just as relevant and useful. Art and design or information management could be helpful to students interested in advertising and marketing.

- Avoid relying on subjects that have little or no relevance to the area of business and commerce (dance, music, physical education), although they could be very helpful as the fifth or sixth subject, especially if they keep you motivated to study and do well at school. And they do contribute to your development as a person.

- Keep your options open by taking some subjects that will allow you to change your direction if you find that accountancy is not your passion after all, or your early dreams of running the World Trade Organisation have to be scaled down to more realistic plans.

- It is important that you do your best and achieve the highest possible grades. It is not just the total number of credits that matters (although it pays to be strategic about that too). The quality and depth of your learning are important, along with the skills and confidence you will be able to take with you to university.

5
BUILDER, PLUMBER, SOLDIER, CHEF?

INTRODUCTION

Needing to do well at school and achieve UE and NCEA Level 3 Certificate is not only for the top students and those aiming to attend university. The last 3 years of high school are your opportunity to get a solid grounding in the knowledge and skills you will need in practically any further education, work or career. Things such as the ability to think clearly, find the information you need, solve problems, express yourself effectively (verbally, and in writing in different situations), mathematical skills, and a basic understanding of science—all these things will help you after you leave school. So don't think that because all you want is to be a builder or a plumber, or to join the army, you don't need to study maths or science or do well in English or history.

Yet again, the best piece of advice anyone can give you is to keep your options open while at school. There is no harm in having 20 Level 3 credits in maths, or drama, or English, if at the end of school you decide that you want to be a fashion designer. You might in fact find these subjects very helpful. But if you don't keep your options open and choose instead a poorly planned mix of subjects, and in your last year at school decide to go on to university, lack of those academic subjects could be a serious barrier.

Something like this happened to Peter, who was ready to leave school at the end of Year 12 to become an electrician, like his older brother. A long conversation with an uncle during the summer holidays convinced him that he should go back to school, get the advanced maths and physics under his belt, and aim to enrol at university to study electrical engineering. The fact that he had not done enough of the right standards in maths in Year 12 became a major problem. It took a lot of convincing of the heads of maths and science at his school to allow him to take Level 3 calculus and physics, both of which are needed for entry to a degree in engineering. Peter was successful, although he had to work extremely hard to make up for the gap in his maths preparation. With his engineering degree almost completed, his career prospects now include designing electronic equipment, from large-scale power-generating wind- or water-driven turbines, to electronic circuitry for gadgets (from mobile phones to jumbo jets), to nanotechnology used in medicine and other fields.

APPRENTICESHIPS

Had he continued with his original plan, Peter would still have benefited from the study of maths and other subjects, because apprenticeships (at National Certificate Levels 2, 3 or 4) involve not only on-the-job training and skill assessment, but also evening classes, block courses, or distance education programmes that cover the more theoretical and technical aspects of training. Such courses are offered through polytechnics or industry training organisations (ITOs), and invariably include assessments in the form of written assignments, tests and exams.

EMPLOYERS GENERALLY EXPECT STUDENTS TO HAVE COMPLETED YEAR 12 AND ATTAINED NCEA LEVEL 2

Although entry into apprenticeships is open, employers generally expect students to have completed Year 12 and attained NCEA Level 2. The training organisations usually expect students to have "a good understanding of written and oral English" as well as mathematics and science. Evaluations of various apprenticeship programmes have shown that students without any NCEA qualifications are the least likely to complete their apprenticeships and more likely to fail because of poor literacy and numeracy skills. Students with a Year 12 (NCEA Level 2) qualification have the best success rates.

One way of testing whether work in a particular trade or occupation is for you is to use the opportunities provided through Trades Academies and the Gateway programme. These allow senior secondary school students (Years 11 to 13) to undertake structured learning in the workplace while continuing their study at school. Workplace learning is assessed using unit standards that can contribute to NCEA as well as to industry-specific qualifications. The value of such experiences lies in the hands-on, practical learning that some students find interesting and worthwhile, as well as in the opportunities to experience what working in a particular industry or occupation might be like. Students who show interest and diligence in the workplace might well be offered an apprenticeship with that company or employer. As well as traditional trades such as carpentry, plumbing or hairdressing, Gateway programmes can facilitate access to workplace learning in fields such as banking, retail or web design.

Recently, the Ministry of Education has launched a new initiative called **Vocational Pathways**. It is intended to help students plan their NCEA Level 2 and other qualifications when their goals on leaving school include getting a job or training as an apprentice. Schools can use the pathways to plan courses that are clearly linked to one of the five broad areas:

- Manufacturing and Technology (e.g., furniture making or boat building)
- Construction and Infrastructure (e.g., building or plumbing)
- Primary Industries (e.g., dairy farming or forestry)
- Service Industries (e.g., cooking or hairdressing), and
- Social and Community Services (e.g., first aid or tikanga practices).

Students can choose one of these pathways and include specified courses, called "sector related standards" alongside their NCEA subjects. If you meet the literacy and numeracy requirements at Level 1 and complete 60 Level 2 credits, with at least 20 of the credits from the sector related standards linked to one of the pathways, you can have that pathway recorded on your Record of Achievement. There are two advantages: you can complete practical courses such as farming or building and get credits for them while still at school, without having to pay course fees, and when you apply for a job you will be able to show that you have some relevant skills. Students aiming to complete apprenticeships can complete many of the theoretical courses while still at school, thus reducing the studies they will need to complete later.

Currently there are over 20 **Trades Academies** operating in New Zealand. They are a partnership between schools, tertiary Institutions such as polytechnics, industry training organisations and employers. Trades academies work in conjunction with Vocational Pathways to help students achieve at least NCEA Level 2 and, at the same time, to work towards a Level 1, 2, or 3 National Certificate in a chosen field.

Career advisors in your school will have more information about Trades Academies and Vocational Pathways. You can also get more Information from http://youthguarantee.net.nz/

Eru

Eru followed a path towards an apprenticeship and used the Gateway programme to decide if this was a good choice for him. His older sister had just finished a degree in early childhood education, but Eru felt that his talents lay in more hands-on, physically active work.

A PATH TOWARDS AN APPRENTICESHIP

His father was a pretty good handyman and Eru enjoyed helping him put up a new fence last summer and repair their neighbours' garage after the big storm a few months ago damaged the roof and window.

A good swimmer since a very young age, Eru enjoyed competing in swimming at school and as part of the surf life-saving club during the summer holidays. He was a conscientious student at school but rather shy when it came to speaking up in class. His Year 11 programme was as follows.

YEAR 11 NCEA SUBJECTS	COMMENTS
Level 1 English	Compulsory at this level. It is important to achieve literacy credits for NCEA Level 1, and to meet the prerequisites for more advanced study in English and related subjects at Level 2.
Level 1 Mathematics	Compulsory at this level. It is important to achieve numeracy credits for NCEA Level 1, and to meet the prerequisites for more advanced study in maths and related subjects at Level 2.
Level 1 Science	Compulsory at this level (at Eru's school).
Level 1 Building, construction, and allied trades skills	Optional subject. Unit standards contribute to NCEA Level 1 and towards a National Certificate in Building, Construction and Allied Trades Skills. This is usually a prerequisite for a Level 2 subject in construction skills.
Level 1 Graphics & design	Optional subject. This is relevant preparation for apprenticeship in construction.

Eru achieved NCEA Level 1 at the end of Year 11, including 14 credits in English and 16 in maths—enough to progress to Level 2 in these subjects and more than the required minimum for entry to an apprenticeship. His parents were very pleased with his achievements and encouraged him to continue doing well at school. In Year 12 Eru wanted to get more hands-on experience in the workplace and applied for the Gateway programme. His subjects for Year 12 included the following.

YEAR 12 NCEA SUBJECTS	COMMENTS
Level 2 English	Compulsory at this level. English is important for continuing the development of critical thinking, writing and presentation skills.
Level 2 Mathematics	Compulsory at this level. Maths is very relevant to work in carpentry and construction.
Level 2 Building, construction, and allied trades skills	Unit standards contribute to NCEA Level 2 and towards a National Certificate in Building, Construction and Allied Trades Skills.
Level 2 Graphics & design	Optional subject. This is an appropriate choice for a student aiming for apprenticeship in carpentry or building, but is also helpful in keeping open the option for university study in architecture or design.
Gateway programme	This programme involves workplace-based learning, with the opportunity to complete unit standards in industry-specific knowledge and skills.

By working diligently and completing internal assessments during the year, Eru had no difficulties achieving NCEA Level 2. He also achieved a number of credits with Merit in maths and in graphics & design. The Gateway experience and the work he did in building & construction and graphics & design subjects confirmed for him his plans to undertake an apprenticeship in carpentry. The question at the end of Year 12 was whether to leave school at this point or return for a further year.

In the end Eru chose the practical way of dealing with this question. If he was able to secure a job with a training agreement, he would leave school and begin his apprenticeship. If not, he would return to school and use it to complete further unit standards in construction skills and graphic design, as well as Level 3 standards in English and maths. If he ever decided to undertake a diploma or degree in construction management at a polytechnic or university, these subjects would stand him in good stead.

Eru was able to get employment with a local builder and commence his apprenticeship. He will need to achieve nearly 300 Level 3 and 4 credits, through some 8,000 hours of practical work and study, over 4 to 5 years. At the end of this time Eru will be a fully qualified builder, with a nationally recognised certificate or diploma.

ARMED SERVICES

One way of completing an apprenticeship in a variety of fields, from carpentry to vehicle mechanics, is by joining the armed services, undergoing a basic training course and then doing a more extended period of trade training. The majority of school leavers will not take this option, but it might suit some who wish to join the armed services and who might find the structured, communal nature of service life helpful in their work and training.

> *THE ARMY WILL NEED EVIDENCE THAT YOU ARE AT LEAST 17 YEARS OF AGE, PHYSICALLY FIT AND HEALTHY, HAVE NO CRIMINAL CONVICTIONS, AND ARE SUITED TO A CAREER IN THE ARMED FORCES*

Some secondary schools now offer a services academy option. Not all students taking part will go on to join the armed services, and others who do not participate in the academy while at school might still do so, either on leaving school or later. Places at each academy are usually limited to about 20 students. Academy activities include an induction course at the Waiouru Army Camp before the start of the school year, and regular, usually outdoor, activities supervised by armed services staff. In addition, academy students have to be enrolled in normal NCEA study at school.

For some students this might be a good way of seeing how they respond to the structured and sometimes quite strict demands associated with being part of the armed services. It does not commit you to joining the army; in fact, the main aim of the academy is to motivate students to remain at school and learn as much as they can, academically and in terms of practical skills.

If you are considering joining the armed services as a way of furthering your education or training, remember that there are two levels of entry. One is for training as an **ordinary soldier**; the other is for **officer training**. These require different levels of educational achievement. In addition, there are a number of conditions that applicants for basic or officer training in the armed services need to meet that are not normally required for similar education or training in civilian life. The army will need evidence that you are at least 17 years of age, physically fit and healthy, have no criminal convictions, and are suited to a career in the armed forces (a team player, able to take initiative and follow orders, and have good interpersonal communication skills). For officer training there are the added expectations of strong academic skills and leadership qualities (as evidenced in being dux of your school, sports team captain, cultural group leader, or president of a club or society).

Apprenticeships through the armed services require similar levels of academic achievement to apprenticeships undertaken through other providers. English, maths and science are generally required, and for many technical areas graphics and workshop technology might be an advantage.

Apprenticeships are not the only training options offered by the armed services. New recruits may train for **army combat or navy operations work**, including as gunner, marine engineer, diver or helicopter pilot. Or they may **train in support areas**, from logistics (ensuring the supply of materials, communication and other services that support army units in the field and allow navy vessels to operate for prolonged periods at sea), to catering and hospitality, and specialist positions including musicians, education officers, dental assistants and administrators. Most of the apprenticeships and training for support roles can be done in-house, following acceptance into the armed services.

In other cases armed services might:

- support their staff to complete specialist educational programmes, including university degrees (e.g., in economics, law, psychology or engineering)

- recruit current students (e.g., senior medical students, who are supported to complete their medical training before being commissioned as medical officers)

- recruit fully qualified professionals such as registered nurses, surgeons, dentists, lawyers or chaplains.

Billy

Billy and his family live in a small Northland town. His father died in a car accident when Billy was 10 and his mother has struggled to support the family. They have moved several times in the last few years, initially to be closer to Billy's grandparents, and then in search of work and affordable accommodation. This has meant changing schools and having to make new friends—experiences that Billy found unsettling. The situation was made worse when his mother's new partner moved in a couple of years ago. His two younger sisters seem to get on with their stepfather, but somehow Billy manages to rub him the wrong way, even when he tries hard not to. They hardly ever talk to each other, which upsets Billy's mum, but that's just the way things are.

> *THREE THINGS BILLY WANTS: TO LEAVE HOME, TO JOIN THE ARMY, AND TO BECOME A CHEF!*

Billy's way of coping has been to retreat to a secret place—a quiet corner of the local library in winter and the derelict shed at the bottom of their garden in summer. He likes to read about other people's adventures, climbing the Himalayas, sailing solo around the world, or tracking through Africa. He dreams of having his own adventures, one day.

There are three things Billy wants: to leave home, to join the army, and to become a chef! I guess they are related. He knows he is not ready to face the world on his own just yet, and he doesn't want to make the mistakes his cousin did—joining a gang and getting into heaps of trouble. Although he is not all that interested in combat, the army might just be his way to earn a living, see the world, and do something he will enjoy. And deep down he wants to be part of a group and share his adventures with friends his own age. So this is what Billy did in his first year of NCEA.

YEAR 11 NCEA SUBJECTS	COMMENTS
Level 1 English	Compulsory at this level. It is important to achieve literacy credits for NCEA Level 1, and to meet the prerequisites for more advanced study in English and related subjects at Level 2.
Level 1 Mathematics	Compulsory at this level. It is important to achieve numeracy credits for NCEA Level 1, and to meet the prerequisites for more advanced study in maths and related subjects at Level 2.
Level 1 Science	Compulsory at this level (at Billy's school). Science is an important prerequisite for later studies in chemistry, physics or biology.
Level 1 Physical education	Optional subject. Physical fitness is important for acceptance into the army, so Billy took this subject and played cricket and rugby.
Level 1 Hospitality	Optional subject. Hospitality provides practical experience in food handling and preparation, and helps Billy express some of his creative ideas.

Billy achieved NCEA Level 1 at the end of Year 11. He did particularly well in English (all that reading he did on his own had to help), and in hospitality and physical education. Maths and science did not go as well, but he managed to get 14 credits in each, which meant that he could continue with more advanced-level maths and science in Year 12. He surprised himself by doing really well in rugby, playing on the wing and scoring some memorable tries.

Another option became available in Year 12 when Billy's school was selected to host the services academy. He managed to convince the Year 12 Dean to include him in the first group of students selected for the academy. The prospect of a two-week camp and other trips away appealed to him—it was almost like going on a holiday. His programme for Year 12 included the following.

YEAR 12 NCEA SUBJECTS	COMMENTS
Level 2 English	Compulsory at this level. It is important to achieve literacy credits for UE, and for the continuing development of critical thinking, writing and presentation skills. It helped that Billy enjoyed reading and did well in this subject.
Level 2 Mathematics	Compulsory at this level. Maths with algebra is also essential preparation for more advanced study of statistics and calculus.
Level 2 Physical education	Optional subject. This is a good choice for someone planning to join the army.
Level 2 Hospitality	Optional subject. This is relevant to Billy's interests in cooking and becoming a chef.
Services academy	This gives Billy an opportunity to taste army life and develop his interpersonal and team-working skills.

Even though he completed Year 12 with sufficient credits for NCEA Level 2, and could have left school at that point, Billy considered his future carefully and decided to return to school for another year. He had come through with solid rather than exceptional academic results, but had grown in confidence and was set on joining the army and becoming a chef. There was only one catch! He would not turn 17 until June and would be too young to join the army before then. And of course there was no guarantee that he would be accepted. Staying at school and doing his best in Year 13 would give him better preparation if the army option didn't work out. He had already considered other pathways to becoming a chef.

YEAR 13 NCEA SUBJECTS	COMMENTS
Level 3 English	Reading was still a passion, and Billy enjoyed the challenge of doing well in this subject.
Level 3 Mathematics	Although not an easy subject, Billy was determined to keep going with it, especially in statistics.
Level 3 Physical education	Billy enjoyed the practical side and taking part in competitive sports. At this level he also had the option of training to referee games and to organise sports activities. This could be a plus on his army application.
Level 3 Hospitality	This subject gave him the opportunity to plan menus and supplies for special events, and to learn about the nutritional needs of specific groups such as sports teams.
Gateway programme	This programme combines workplace-based learning with the opportunity to complete unit standards in industry-specific knowledge and skills. (Billy spent most of his time working with a catering company, and he learned a lot about ordering supplies and preparing food in large quantities.)

Through his school and practical experiences Billy confirmed his passion for cooking. He achieved Level 3 NCEA and was successful in his application to join the army and begin his apprenticeship as a chef.

Kate

Kate also hopes to join the armed services, especially after reading the story of the first woman to be made captain of a navy ship in New Zealand. Lieutenant Hansen was only 28 when she was appointed captain of *HMNZS Pukaki* in 2010, after only 5 years in the navy. What an inspiration! Being an officer, in charge of a ship, would be awesome, but first Kate has to get through high school and develop the sort of track record that gets you into a university programme or officer training. She might not quite match Lieutenant Hansen's academic record or sporting abilities, but Kate is determined to do *her* best. She is also keen to push the boundaries, in her case by studying engineering and management.

> BEING AN OFFICER, IN CHARGE OF A SHIP, WOULD BE AWESOME

Having completed Year 11 with outstanding results in English, maths, science, physical education, economics and Spanish, Kate was ready to take on the next challenge. As well as focusing on the academic subjects, she was determined to develop her physical fitness and her leadership skills. She was keen to test herself as a prefect, as well as in more competitive pursuits, including the school netball and cycling teams. She also enjoyed the more social game of touch rugby and enjoyed singing in the school choir. Being organised and using her time well would be critical for juggling all these commitments.

For the next 2 years Kate will need to be careful to keep her academic options open and achieve at a high level. In part this is important in case she decides to enrol at university and apply for officer training later, or take the option of applying for officer training at the end of Year 13, with the hope that the navy will recognise her abilities and potential and support her to study at university as part of her training. Her Year 12 subjects are as follows.

YEAR 12 NCEA SUBJECTS	COMMENTS
Level 2 English	Compulsory at this level. English is important for continuing the development of critical thinking, writing and presentation skills.
Level 2 Mathematics	Compulsory at this level. Mathematics with algebra is also essential preparation for more advanced study of calculus.
Level 2 Physics	This is an optional subject but essential preparation for more advanced study of physics.
Level 2 Economics	Optional subject. Economics is relevant to university study in business and commerce.
Level 2 Spanish	Optional subject. Kate is keen to be proficient in another language.
Level 2 Physical education	Optional subject. It suits Kate's sporting interests and rounds off her choices.

As well as doing well academically, Kate will need to demonstrate other achievements—in sport and leadership. Having chosen her path, Kate is also clear about her Year 13 subject choices. She plans to continue with most of her chosen subjects but will probably drop physical education at this level. This will still leave her with five approved subjects, and she might consider sitting Scholarship exams for at least four of them. At the same time, she is planning to continue playing netball and competing in cycling, and is hoping to be made head prefect. These are her Year 13 subjects.

YEAR 13 NCEA SUBJECTS	COMMENTS
Level 3 English	English is important for continuing the development of critical thinking, writing and presentation skills.
Level 3 Calculus	This is essential preparation for university study in engineering.

Level 3 Physics	Physics is essential preparation for university study in engineering.
Level 3 Economics	Economics is relevant to university study in business and management.
Level 3 Spanish	Kate is keen to be proficient in another language and plans to continue studying Spanish at university.

These are the plans and dreams that are motivating Kate to aim high. Whether she joins the navy immediately after school, or goes to university, might not be entirely her decision, but she wants to be ready for the challenge. Will she be the next woman in New Zealand to captain a navy ship? Only time will tell. But Kate is determined to get as much as she can out of her high school education, and to enjoy the experience.

KEY POINTS

Joining the armed services or getting an apprenticeship does not just happen. It usually works out much better if you know what will be involved and are well prepared for it.

- Learning a trade through an apprenticeship, a polytechnic or even by joining the armed services can be a great career option for many school leavers. But remember that you still need to plan how to get there, and you do need to make the most out of the learning opportunities your school is able to provide.

- Good literacy and maths skills are essential, and ongoing learning is always easier if you have a strong base on which to build new knowledge and understanding. Curiosity, the ability to express yourself verbally and in writing, and good planning are just as important here as they are in other areas of study or work.

- Make the most of the opportunities to gain on-the-job experience and skills through programmes such as Gateway. Treat it as another important subject and be prepared to challenge yourself and learn as much as possible.

- Work on developing independent study skills. You'll need them, especially if you choose an apprenticeship. Evening classes or correspondence/online courses require a lot of motivation and good time management, especially after a hard day's work.

- Keeping your options open is still important, especially if you are not sure what might be possible for you once you leave school. The army might not be recruiting for the trades or specialisations that are of interest to you at the time you are ready to join, so you might need a plan B.

- Even if university is not your aim, diploma and degree courses at polytechnics might be easier to get into—and much easier to succeed in—with strong secondary school preparation. So choose your NCEA subjects wisely and try to achieve to the best of your ability. And never underestimate what hard work and determination can achieve.

6
WHAT PARENTS CAN DO TO HELP

INTRODUCTION

If it "takes a village to raise a child", it takes at least a school and parents and whānau to get a student through their high school years and on the way to further education and a satisfying career. Navigating the NCEA requirements and subject choices, and planning ahead with confidence, can take some doing. We have written this book for parents and whānau as much as for the students.

> If there is one piece of advice we would give you, it would be to learn as much as you can about NCEA and talk with your child and your child's teachers—regularly.

It will take a decade or more before students with experience of NCEA become parents with teenage children embarking on their senior high school years. In the meantime, as parents and whānau, you need to learn what NCEA is all about, how it will affect your children, and how you can best support them to achieve their potential and not waste the opportunities their high school years provide.

In this chapter we are drawing on the experiences of over 40 parents we interviewed as part of our research on students', teachers' and parents' understanding of NCEA. What we found was that parents are often confused about NCEA and unsure how to talk to their children or their children's teachers about it. Many rely on their children for explanations of what "achievement standards", or "approved subjects", or different "versions" of core subjects such as maths or science mean. So if you are feeling a little uncertain, or feel like a complete beginner when it comes to NCEA, you are not alone.

The first thing we would suggest is that you **read Chapter 1**. Although written primarily for students, because they need to understand what NCEA is all about, the information is just as relevant for parents and other interested adults. As we mentioned there, NCEA is both complex and flexible, and that is both its strength and, in some ways, its weakness. There is a lot of information to get through, there are new words like "credits", and there are common words like "standards" and "levels" that have quite specific meanings—or more than one meaning. Hopefully Chapter 1 will help to give you a clear picture of how the system works and help you with the language of NCEA, even if you have to go back to it to refresh your understanding of specific points.

In addition, here are some points to highlight the things that you as a parent/whānau should keep in mind.

GETTING STARTED WITH NCEA

In Term 3 or Term 4 of Year 10 (4th form in the old system), your child will be asked to indicate which subjects he or she would like to do the following year. The school will provide a Curriculum Guide or NCEA Subject Handbook listing the subjects that are available, and this will usually provide information on which subjects are compulsory for all students and which are optional, so that students can choose whether to take art, or woodwork, or drama, or history, or other subjects offered by their school.

YOU NEED TO LEARN WHAT NCEA IS ALL ABOUT

It is a good idea to read through this information carefully, paying particular attention to where each subject can lead in subsequent years and what your child will be able to do as a result of these initial choices. (A sample flow chart of how subjects connect at different levels, and a specific example of science subjects, is provided in Appendix 2 at the end of this book. Your child's school will have a similar chart of the subjects available at their school.)

Talk with your child

If you haven't done so already, or even if you have, the end of Year 10 would be a good time to sit down with your child and have a discussion about their interests, hopes and plans for the future, and the importance of making the most of the learning opportunities at school. Encourage them to take subjects that will help them learn things they might know little about at this stage—be it history, literature, chemistry or another academic subject. Schools are there to teach your children specialised knowledge which they cannot learn on their own or at home.

> SIT DOWN WITH YOUR CHILD AND HAVE A DISCUSSION ABOUT THEIR INTERESTS, HOPES AND PLANS FOR THE FUTURE

Doing subjects they enjoy and find interesting is fine, as long as that is not limited to sport, motor mechanics and fashion design. That's why most schools require students to take English (or te reo Māori), maths (pāngaru) and science (pūtaiao) in their first year of NCEA (Year 11). These subjects provide a strong base from which to build and extend into subjects such as drama, media studies, statistics, biology, chemistry and physics in subsequent years. But they can only do this if the subjects are the appropriate versions, and include standards and the content students need to have as preparation for more advanced study.

Has your child been placed in the appropriate classes for English, maths and science?

At the beginning of Year 11, check to make sure that your child is in the appropriate version of Level 1 English, maths and science classes. Terms such as "academic" or "extension" might be used for classes for academically able students, and "practical" or "applied" for those seen as less able. Sometimes the only indication of different subject versions is in the numbers, such as "Maths 101", "Maths 102" and "Maths 103". Students are allocated to such classes mainly on the basis of previous tests (such as *PAT* or *asTTle*, which they are given in Years 9 and 10), but schools can and do give consideration to other factors.

Being placed in an applied maths or English class is fine for students who are genuinely unable to learn at a higher level. The learning they will undertake will be useful and they will achieve better than in a class where they are made to feel inadequate. All students are capable of learning, but how much and how fast might be quite different.

But if academically able students are placed in a practical or applied maths or science class in Year 11 because they had an unsettled year, or did not consider the tests they had to take in Year 10 to be important, or simply scored poorly in a test, this could have serious consequences. A bright student will become bored in a class that is not stimulating enough, or moving at too slow a pace, and will easily lose motivation and become uninterested in the subject or even in being at school. Another consequence might be that the student is not given the opportunity to study standards (subject components) that are required for more advanced study in that subject in subsequent years, closing off the options to subjects they will need for tertiary study later. A further consequence might be that the subject is not eligible for endorsement. In other words, students can gain credits but only at Achieved level, and not at Merit or Excellence levels needed for endorsement.

> As a parent, you should assure yourself that you know which classes your child has been allocated to, that you and your child understand the implications for the future, and that you and your child agree with this allocation. If not, discuss it with your child's school and make sure that if changes are needed they are made as early as possible. It is much harder to make up for lost learning opportunities a year or two down the track.

Has your child chosen the most appropriate optional subjects?

Talk to your child about the optional subjects he or she wants to do in Year 11, and why. It's great if they want to take geography or history or physics because their friends are taking these subjects, and they will encourage each other to study and do well. Automotive engineering might also be a great choice, but not if the main reason is that "all the rugby boys are doing it, and it will be a chance to chill out and play with car engines".

> *POOR CHOICES ARE EASY TO MAKE BUT CAN BE QUITE HARD TO REMEDY LATER*

If you are not sure if the subjects your child wants to do are the best choices, contact the school and ask to talk with your child's form teacher, Year 11 dean or co-ordinator, or career guidance teacher. Poor choices are easy to make but can be quite hard to remedy later. On the other hand, don't force your children to take subjects they are not interested in or which will lead to career options they will not want to follow. (Accounting is a great subject for a student interested in business or finance, but not for a student who wants to study music, nursing or social work.)

How well do you know your child's school and school rules?

Attend every meeting or information evening your child's school might offer to parents and whānau. Talk to the teachers teaching your child and show them that you are interested in your child's learning and are willing to play your part. Get a sense of how they see your child and what expectations they have in relation to his or her learning and achievement at school. Ask questions and seek information if some things are not clear to you. This can apply especially to the rules each school develops, that are not always written down and are not necessarily easy to understand by parents and others outside the school. Here are some examples.

(a) Some schools require students to take five subjects each year, others six, and some might require six subjects in Years 11 and 12 and five subjects in Year 13. You might prefer that your child maximises his or her learning opportunities and take six subjects, but this will not be possible in a school organised around students taking only five.

(b) Subjects are often organised into groups or bands, and timetables developed in line with such organisation. So you might think it a good idea for your son or daughter to take metalwork and physics, but the timetable might not allow for this particular combination of subjects.

(c) Places in individual classes are limited, so make sure that your child returns his or her subject choice forms on time. Students who are late might be allocated to classes or subjects that still have room, rather than to the classes that are best for them.

(d) Progression to a higher level of study in a subject will depend on prerequisite or entry requirements (sometimes called "subject passes") set by each school. This might include the number of credits at the previous level—as low as 10 in some cases, or as high as 18 in others—or achievement of specific standards and grades (Merit or Excellence). Make sure that you and your child are aware of these prerequisites and are in a good position to meet them.

Keeping an eye on your child's progress

Be aware of how early students start to accumulate NCEA credits from internally assessed assignments and tests and try to monitor your child's progress. How many credits are they expected to have gained in each subject by the end of each school term, and are they on target or falling behind? Keep in mind that some subjects tend to have mostly internal assessments (and will be able to give you an indication of credits gained over time), and others have mostly end-of-year external assessments, so the majority of credits in these subjects will not be gained until the end of the year.

Your child should also be tracking his or her own progress, and the school should send periodic (at least twice a year) reports informing you of your child's achievement and any issues of concern to the school. If you are not receiving this information, again, contact the school and make sure that you know how well your child is doing. (Before you do that, check that the report is not in your child's school bag!)

The importance of homework and good study habits

Check what homework or other set work your child is required to complete, and how any such work relates to internal assessments or to building up a portfolio (a collection of art or other work) for external assessment. Failure to submit required work might mean not achieving any credits for that standard or component of a subject, as well as not learning important content.

If you are not confident or able to discuss the details of what your child is studying or required to complete as part of homework or independent study, make sure that you at least provide the time and space needed for such tasks. If your school provides lunchtime or after-school homework centres or tutorials for students who need such support, encourage your child to attend and make use of the teachers who are there to guide and assist students in their work.

Encourage your children to develop good study habits and to set high goals for their own learning. Because NCEA is flexible, students do not have to sit every test or do every assignment. They can choose to focus on some and leave out others. This makes it easy for students to put off submitting work for internal assessments. Students might also be tempted to submit work that is not of a high enough standard, knowing that within the NCEA system they will be given another chance to resubmit the work. Such practices need to be discouraged, especially because rules around resubmissions and "re-sits" of internal assessments have been tightened so that students now get only one chance to be reassessed on work they have failed previously.

The importance of external exams

> Make sure that your child prepares for end-of-year exams, turns up at the appointed times, and uses all the available time to answer the questions to the best of his or her ability.

Students learn to be street-smart in relation to NCEA, without necessarily appreciating the full consequences of their actions, or telling their families what they are doing and why. Some will not study for external exams, might fail to attend, or might walk out after an hour because they know that they have enough internally earned credits for a pass in that subject. You need to be aware of this possibility and not accept comments such as "I've already passed that subject" without further discussion.

Some students might lack confidence in relation to exams and get into a habit of avoiding external assessments. This can have serious consequences for their learning and achievement: first, because they might fail to achieve enough credits overall, and secondly, because many of the credits achieved with Merit and Excellence come from external assessments. And if they plan to go to university, lack of exam skills will be a real disadvantage, because most first-year university papers include exams.

The importance of support and praise

As much as possible, encourage your children to manage their time well, to put in their best work each time, and to aim to achieve with Merit and Excellence and not settle for the minimum required to only just meet the passing standard. *Praise your children when they do well.* It is amazing what a difference positive feedback can make to a child's motivation and sense of self worth!

If you are satisfied with your child's subject choices and class allocations, have a good understanding of the progress he or she should be making and know how to contact the school if you have any concerns, then you are already doing a lot to support your child to succeed.

MAKING NCEA WORK FOR YOUR CHILD

Continue to talk with your child

Most students will need guidance and support during the first year of NCEA, but should be able to take on greater responsibility for their choices and performance at school as they mature and gain more experience. Even so, you should keep a watchful eye on what your child is doing at school and how well he or she is achieving. NCEA should be the topic of ongoing conversations you have with your child. Here are some questions you might use.

(a) What are you learning in science/maths/history, etc? Which subjects or topics are you enjoying, and which ones not? Are you having any difficulties with what the teachers expect of you?

(b) Are you achieving the credits in line with the goals we've discussed at the beginning of the year? Have you had to resubmit any of your work or re-sit an assessment? How did you feel about that? Do you know how to achieve on the first attempt and avoid re-sits? Have you discussed this with your teacher? Do you need more help?

(c) If you are having any difficulties, what do you think the reasons are? What can you do to help yourself? Have you talked with your teachers about this? If yes, did it help? If not, would it help if I came with you and we talked with the teacher together? Is there anything else we (parents/whānau) can do to help? (Some teenagers might not like to have their parents involved in what is happening at school, but don't be put off contacting the school if you think it is necessary.)

(d) What are your best subjects this year? Are they related to what you would like to study/do after you leave school? What other subjects are important if you want to achieve this goal? How well are you doing in those subjects?

(e) When do you need to start preparing for exams? What material do you need to cover? Have you practised answering exam questions from last year? How well did you understand the questions? How confident did you feel that you could organise your thoughts, plan what to write, and write all that you needed in the time you were given?

(f) Given this year's experience, what subjects would you like to do next year? Are these the subjects you will need for the following year (or for tertiary education)?

(g) Have your goals changed or become clearer? Does this change anything you should be doing at school?

IF YOU HAVE CONCERNS, TALK WITH YOUR CHILD'S TEACHERS

No doubt you will have other questions. The important thing is to talk with your child often and in a way that is supportive so that you know whether your child is doing well, enjoying school, having difficulties with a particular subject, and receiving (or not receiving) the help he or she needs. If you have concerns, talk with your child's teachers.

Choosing subjects for Year 12

The choice of Year 12 (NCEA Level 2) subjects is particularly important. Only one or two subjects might be compulsory, so there is more scope to choose or be guided into subjects that might or might not keep your child on the most appropriate educational pathway.

Encourage your children to **consider each subject choice carefully** and help them to appreciate the need for balance in terms of subjects they would *like* to do and subjects they *need* to do. It's great if these are the same, but there is often one subject (or two) that might be more challenging than others, might require a lot more effort, or involves a teacher the student doesn't like or finds unhelpful. The easy way out—dropping the subject and picking up an easier alternative (like a Level 1 subject)—is not usually a wise decision in the long run, so try to work through the issues with your child and negotiate a more effective strategy.

You might find it helpful to read through some of the stories in Chapters 2, 3, 4 and 5. They might help you see how subject choices in Year 12 can work for some students and fail to work for other students. Watch out for the traps of collecting too many Level 1 credits, or doing subjects that are not required as prerequisites for future studies or subjects that lead away from the long-term goals you and your child see as important.

Aiming high and finding the right balance

Help your children to set medium-term goals, such as how many credits they should be aiming to achieve in each subject and in which subjects they should aim to work towards Merit and Excellence. Course and Certificate endorsements do not just happen because a student is particularly bright. They are earned by hard and consistent work, including strong preparation and performance in external exams. If your children's work includes a portfolio (collection) of work for external assessment (in art, graphics, technology or another subject), make sure they are working on it throughout the year and not leaving everything to the last minute.

Discuss other interests your children have and activities they are engaged in at school, and how these fit into their overall time schedules and plans. Sporting, cultural, music, debating and leadership activities such as being a prefect can all enrich your children's experience of school, and contribute to their development as confident and well-rounded persons.

WATCH OUT FOR THE TRAP OF COLLECTING TOO MANY LEVEL 1 CREDITS

Young people thrive on positive feedback, be it applause for their school play or kapa haka performance, winning a sports competition, or being selected to captain a team or be a senior prefect. But be careful that such activities do not take over and become all consuming for your child. This might be a particular risk for academically able students in smaller schools, where various leadership roles are shared among a small number of students. Being the head prefect, captain of the first XV, president of the student council and student representative on the Board of Trustees are all wonderful recognitions of a student's talents and abilities, but should not come at the expense of Certificate endorsement with Excellence or achieving a Scholarship award. Watch out especially that the organisation of end-of-year activities such as the school play or senior ball does not cut into essential study and preparation for end-of-year exams.

The right time to leave school

If your child is considering leaving school at the end of Year 12, help him or her review all the pros and the cons of that decision.

(a) Will they have achieved NCEA Level 2 by the end of the year? (If not, is it wise to leave school without it?)

(b) Do they have a definite plan and good prospects for what they want to do—an apprenticeship or a job lined up, or acceptance into a certificate or diploma course in a polytechnic they cannot do at school? (If not, might it not be wiser to go back to school?)

(c) Could they take non-NCEA courses they are interested in through the school, including through a trade academy or Gateway programme, which are free to high school students, rather than through polytechnics or industry/private training organisations, which charge fees?

(d) Do they hope to attend university in a year or two, after they have gained some work experience, earned some money or travelled? They will still need to meet the entry requirements, so not having achieved UE and NCEA Level 3 will be a real barrier. Even entry after the age of 20 is based on evidence of past academic achievement and the potential to cope with university study and is not guaranteed.

(e) What is the main reason they want to leave school at this stage? Consider issues such as peer pressure, bullying or disagreements with a teacher. There are other ways of dealing with these matters than leaving school.

Making the most of Year 13

If your child is staying at school through to Year 13, help him or her set clear goals for the year and make sure these are achievable through the study programme the school will provide.

Students who have failed to achieve NCEA Level 2 in Year 12 can achieve it in Year 13. Those who have failed by a small number of credits can achieve both NCEA Level 2 and Level 3 in their final year. This is one of the advantages of NCEA: allowing students to take courses (or specific standards within courses) at different levels in the same year.

> STUDENTS WHO ARE ON TRACK AND HAVE DONE WELL IN PREVIOUS YEARS SHOULD BE IN A GOOD POSITION TO ACHIEVE BOTH NCEA LEVEL 3 AND UE IN YEAR 13

On the other hand, students who are on track and have done well in previous years should be in a good position to achieve both NCEA Level 3 and UE in Year 13. And students who have excelled in their studies to this point might also be able to gain New Zealand Scholarship awards. That might seem like a lot to aim for and achieve in a single year, but it is perfectly possible, especially because achievement of UE and NCEA Level 3 can be based on the same subjects and the same work. It will take careful planning, hard work and determination by the student, and the understanding and support of the school and parents/whānau, especially to achieve a Scholarship award on top of other qualifications, but you can only achieve something if you try.

If your child is aiming to go to university

If your child is aiming to go to university, the start of Year 13 is your final chance to check the entry requirements for the university and the degree programme he or she wants to attend. Make sure that you, your child, and your child's teachers are all aware of any specific subject and credit requirements (e.g., at least 18 credits in Level 3 chemistry and biology for pharmacy, or at least 17 external Level 3 credits in calculus and physics for engineering) for the university to which your child will apply. Make sure that all the required subjects are available to your child, and that they are eligible for endorsement with Merit or Excellence.

Sometimes a school is unable to teach a particular subject your child needs because it does not have a teacher qualified to teach a particular subject at this level, or because there are only one or two students in the school who want to take that particular subject. You need to be aware of this, preferably before the start of the school year, so that you can consider other options.

One option might be to access the subject through correspondence. This can be quite challenging for a student without experience of distance or extramural study. At the very least it requires the student to be very organised and self-disciplined in order to keep up the required study. It also requires the student to be confident enough to initiate contact with correspondence school teachers and seek help from people he or she does not know and might never meet in person. You should discuss your child's needs with the school and ask questions such as:

(a) How many other students (if any) are being offered the correspondence option in this subject?

(b) What resources will be available to my child (e.g., access to laboratory equipment for chemistry or physics)?

(c) Who among the teachers will be available to provide advice and support (in terms of subject content and monitoring that my child is making adequate progress)?

(d) What other support mechanisms might be available (e.g., joining students at another school for some of the time, or, if you can afford it, finding a private tutor)?

If you decide that correspondence is your best (or only) option, keep a particularly close watch on how your child is doing in this subject during the year. If you have concerns, discuss them with the school and ask for help while there is time to remedy the situation. **Encourage your child to take increasing responsibility** for his or her decisions, including on issues such as:

(a) how many extra approved subjects (above the required minimum for UE) to take

(b) whether to aim for Certificate endorsement or sit for Scholarship awards

(c) what extracurricular activities to choose and how to balance his or her overall commitments

(d) how to prepare for transition to university (apply for scholarships, arrange accommodation if moving away from home, check out enrolment procedures and prepare the necessary documents, apply for a student allowance or loan, etc).

Make sure your child uses every opportunity to find out about university study and the available careers. School trips to university open days can be especially valuable, particularly for students from rural communities or those with no previous contact with universities. Sitting in on a typical lecture, meeting university lecturers and professors, or talking with senior students or recent graduates in the field of your child's interest can be very helpful.

KEY POINTS

- Just because it might be new and complicated, don't be intimidated by NCEA, and don't be afraid to ask questions if some aspect is not clear to you.

- Talk with your children and learn with them and from them as they become used to working within the NCEA system.

- Talk with your children's school and attend parent–teacher conferences, meetings and information sessions.

- At the beginning of each year make sure that you and your child are satisfied with the subjects he or she selects and is able to take. If not, seek to change the situation as early as possible and, if necessary, be persistent in your dealings with the school.

- Be aware of how much internal and external assessment is involved in each subject your child is taking and what progress you can expect to see in terms of credit gains by the end of each school term. Keep a watch not only on the number of credits but also on the level of achievement (Achieved, Merit, Excellence), and on any areas where the work was not submitted, or there was a need for a re-sit, and what the outcome was.

- Remember the new grades and their abbreviations: A means "Achieved" (not has come top of the class); there are no Bs, Cs, or Ds. M stands for "Merit" and indicates performance above the minimum standard for a pass, and E stands for "Excellence" and indicates outstanding effort and achievement.

- Don't hesitate to intervene if you have concerns about your child's progress or any specific issues that are not helping his or her learning. Ask to see the appropriate subject teacher, form teacher or dean and seek their advice and help.

- Encourage your child to monitor and track his or her own performance through NCEA, and adjust study habits or seek help if falling behind short-term goals, such as 12 credits in maths by the end of the second term.

- Praise and celebrate your children's academic as well as other achievements and encourage them to do their best.

APPENDIX
1

Figure A1.1 A sample flow chart of subjects and links between different years and NCEA levels as developed by Kaitaia College

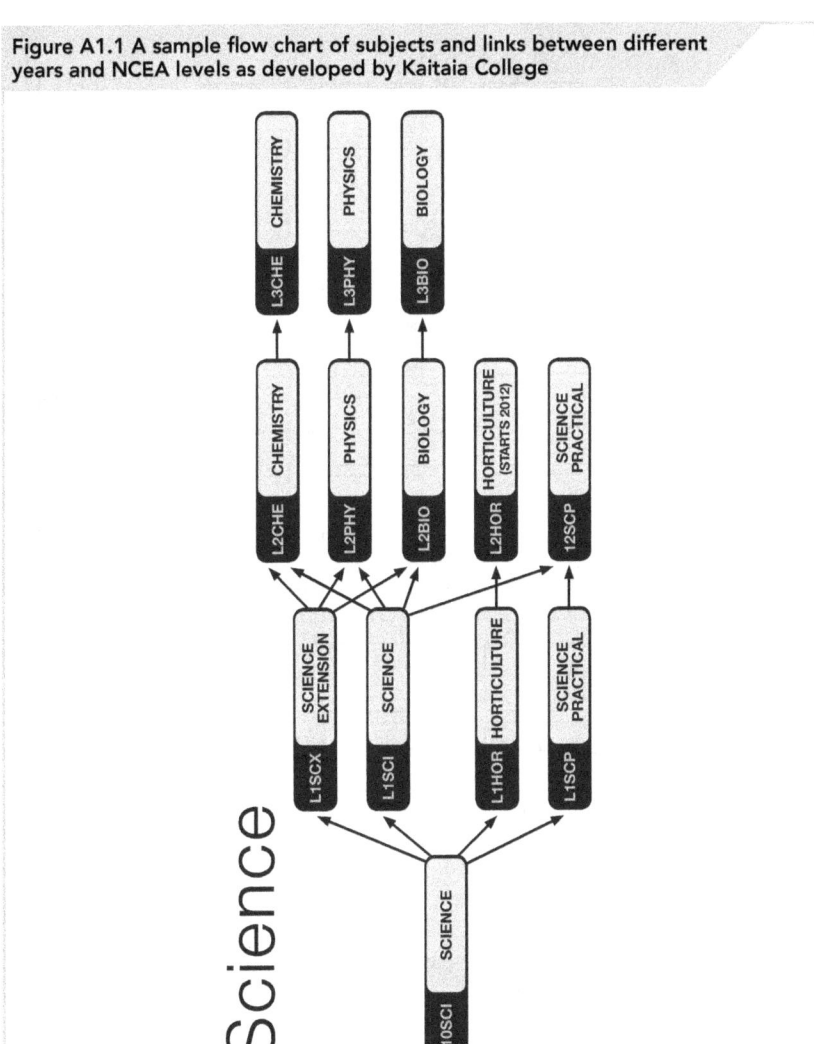

FIGURE A1.2 A sample flow chart of subjects and links between different years and NCEA levels as developed by Kaitaia College

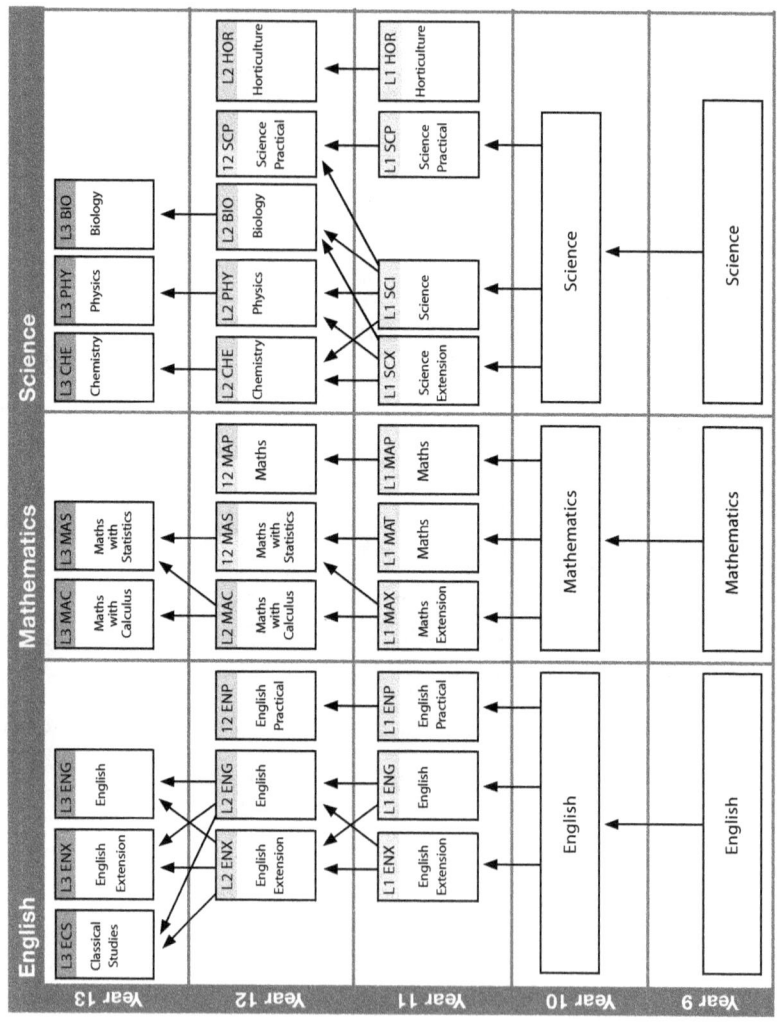

134 // UNDERSTANDING NCEA

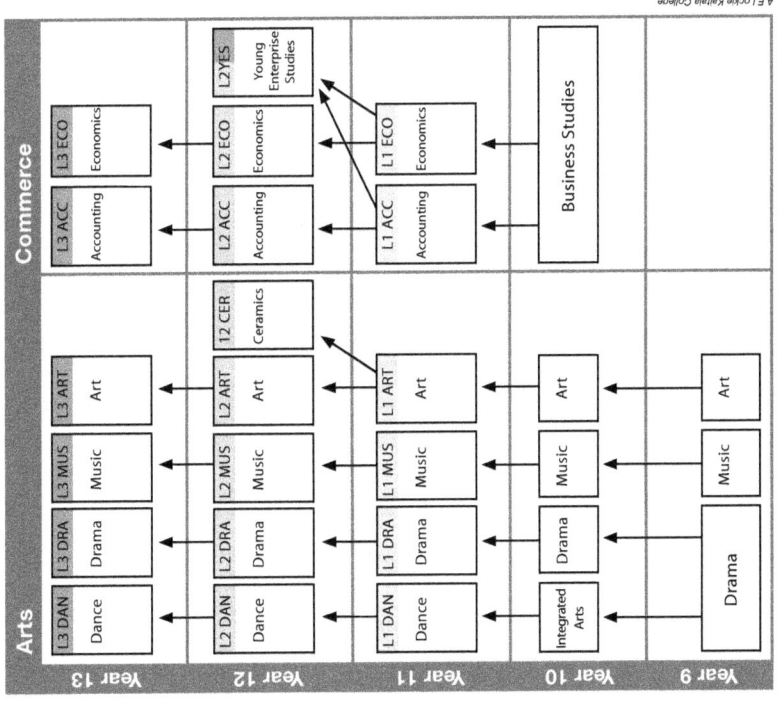

A E Lockie Kaitaia College

APPENDIX 1 // 135

FIGURE A1.2 (cont.) A sample flow chart of subjects and links between different years and NCEA levels as developed by Kaitaia College

Kaitaia College Curriculum Overview
(cont.)

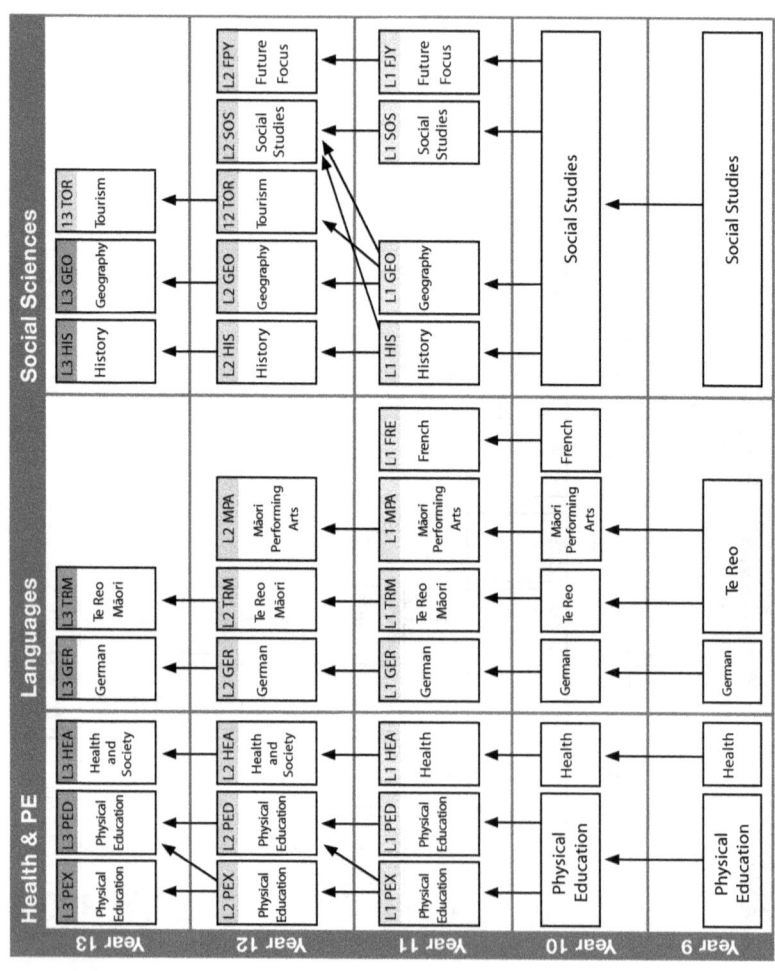

This information must be viewed with individual subject information and flow charts.
Please note that there will be a minimum number of pupils required in order for a course to be taught.

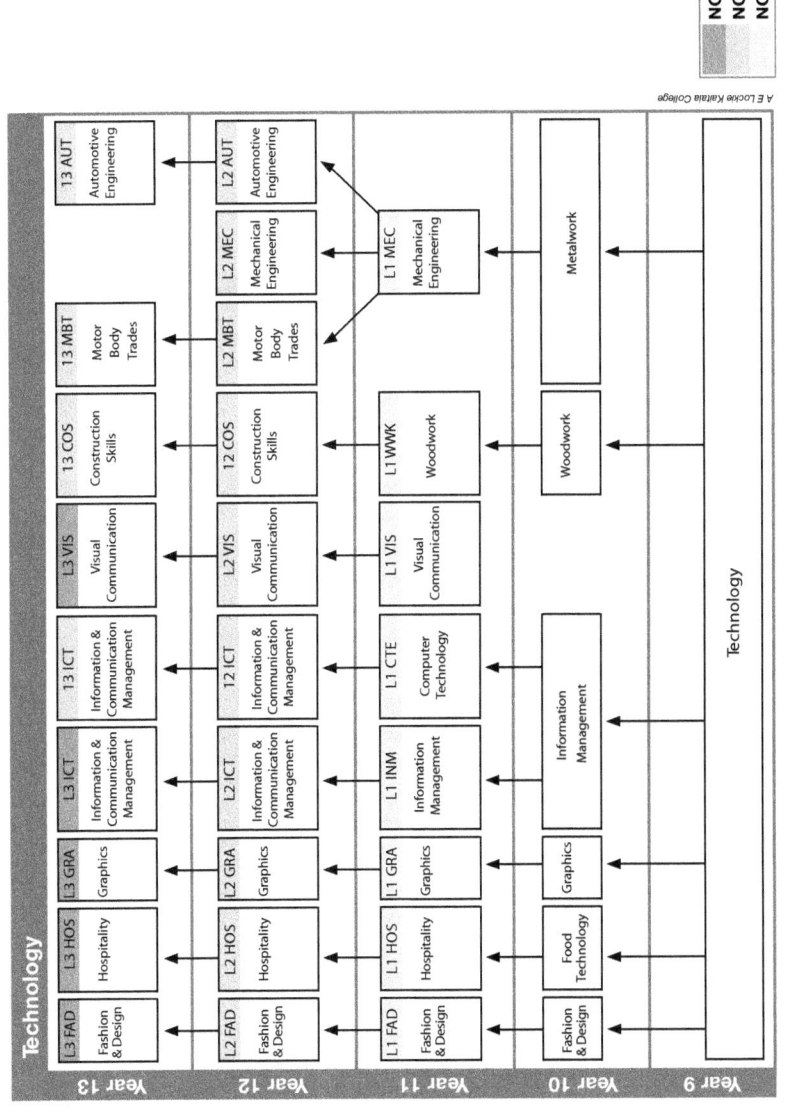

APPENDIX 1 // 137

APPENDIX 2

SIGNIFICANT STANDARDS FOR PROGRESSION TO HIGHER LEVELS WITHIN CORE SUBJECTS OF ENGLISH, MATHEMATICS AND SCIENCE

Because NCEA allows schools to construct individual subjects from a large number of standards (smaller subject components), the content of a subject such as maths or science can differ between schools. More importantly, a school will usually offer different versions of the core subjects of English, maths and science, but made up of slightly (or significantly) different standards. A Level 1 maths course, for example, might or might not include algebra or geometry. Or a Level 1 science course might include biology, physics or chemistry, but not necessarily all of these.

If you plan to attend university (or undertake degree-level study at a polytechnic), make sure the core subject versions you are taking in Year 11 (and 12) are made up of the appropriate standards (see Table A2.1) and that at least half of these standards are externally assessed. This will ensure that you will meet the prerequisite requirements for progression to higher levels of study (NCEA Levels 2 and 3), and have the most relevant and helpful preparation for university study in these or related subjects.

Because each school is free to decide how to structure its subjects and what prerequisites to set for progression to higher-level study, it is really important that you check this information with your school and are satisfied that you have been allocated to the most appropriate class for each of these courses.

Table A2.1: Significant NCEA standards for progression to higher-level studies

SUBJECT/COURSE	NOTES	IMPORTANT CONTENT
Mathematics	Maths is treated as compulsory in most New Zealand schools in Year 11, but content can vary between schools and within the same school offering different versions of the same subject.	In Year 11 make sure your course includes algebra, number, statistics and geometry achievement standards at Level 1. This is important for later study of calculus and statistics. In Year 12 make sure your course includes achievement standards that cover algebra, graphs, and calculus skills at Level 2.
English / te reo Māori	English or te reo Māori is treated as compulsory in most New Zealand schools in Year 11. It is also compulsory in Year 12 in many schools (to allow students to meet UE literacy requirements).	Make sure your course includes creative as well as transactional writing, reading and comprehension skills, literature study skills, and research techniques. To progress to higher levels of study it is especially important that you perform well in the creative* and the transactional** writing elements of the course.

| Science | This subject is compulsory in some, but not all, New Zealand schools in Year 11. This can be "general science", including standards from different branches of science; or it can be a specialised subject such as biology, chemistry, physics or astronomy. (Note: geography is often defined as a science subject but does not provide appropriate preparation for more advanced study of chemistry, physics or biology, or for university study in medicine or engineering, although it is a useful general education subject.) | **For more advanced study of biology** In Level 3 biology there is a particular emphasis on genetics, so to progress through to Level 3 biology you will need to demonstrate knowledge of genetics at Level 1 of the biology (or general science) course, and at Level 2 of the biology course. Schools usually require a minimum of 12–16 credits from the previous level of study, including the genetics standard for progress to Level 3. **For more advanced study of chemistry** Schools usually require 12–16 credits from the previous level of study for progress to the next level of study, and may require achievement with Merit for the chemistry standard in the Year 11 general science course. **For more advanced study of physics** Schools usually require that students have done well in the physics standard of the Level 1 science course, and to have done well in the algebra and graphs sections of the maths course, to be accepted into Level 2 physics, and to be able to progress to Level 3. For students going on to study engineering at university, important Level 2 and 3 physics standards include mechanics and electricity. |

* Creative writing includes use of personal imagination to write short stories, essays, poetry or other pieces that reflect personal feelings or experience.
** Transactional writing refers to more formal styles of writing that depend on reasoning, logic, explanation and factual accounts, such as technical reports.

APPENDIX 3

USEFUL WEBSITES AND SOURCES OF FURTHER INFORMATION

General sources

New Zealand Qualifications Authority (NZQA): useful for help in understanding NCEA

http://www.nzqa.govt.nz/qualifications-standards/qualifications/ncea/understanding-ncea/

Check the NZQA website for updates on information about NCEA, including course and certificate endorsements, the list of approved subjects for UE, UE regulations, New Zealand Scholarship awards, and related information.

Careers Services: for secondary students and school leavers

http://www.careers.govt.nz/plan-your-career/

Check the Careers Services website for information about a wide range of jobs and careers, and the related educational requirements.

Youth Guarantee: useful information about Vocational Pathways and Trades Academies

http://youthguarantee.net.nz/

Check the Youth Guarantee website for specific subjects and assessment standards related to different vocational pathways.

Unibound: Stories of Students Transitioning from School to University (book)

Online purchase at:
http://www.nzcer.org.nz/books

This book includes 15 stories written by students who have made a transition from school to university, some more successfully than others, as well as some general advice about managing the transition experience.

School career advisers

Ask about this at your school. Career advisers have a lot of information (printed and electronic) about different careers and tertiary education programmes. They can advise you on the NCEA subjects that will prepare you for further education or work in specific fields.

New Zealand university websites (information for prospective students)

Auckland University of Technology
http://www.aut.ac.nz/study-at-aut/entry-requirements

The University of Auckland
http://www.education.auckland.ac.nz/uoa/home/for/future-undergraduates

University of Waikato
http://www.waikato.ac.nz/study

Massey University
http://www.massey.ac.nz/massey/prospective/

Victoria University of Wellington
http://www.victoria.ac.nz/home/admisenrol

University of Canterbury
http://www.canterbury.ac.nz/prospectivestudents.shtml

Lincoln University
http://www.lincoln.ac.nz/Studying-at-Lincoln/

University of Otago
http://www.otago.ac.nz/prospectivestudents/

Polytechnic/institute of technology websites

These institutions offer degree qualifications in nursing, business, tourism, Māori studies, arts and other areas, as well as a range of diploma and certificate courses, including trades training courses. Many also have campuses in locations other than their main campus (shown below).

North Tec: Whangarei
http://www.northtec.ac.nz/

Unitec: West Auckland
http://www.unitec.ac.nz/

Manukau Institute of Technology: South Auckland
http://www.manukau.ac.nz/

Waikato Institute of Technology: Hamilton
http://www.wintec.ac.nz/

Waiariki Institute of Technology: Rotorua
http://www.waiariki.ac.nz/

Eastern Institute of Technology: Hawke's Bay (including Tairawhiti Polytechnic in Gisborne)
http://www.eit.ac.nz/

Western Institute of Technology: New Plymouth
http://www.witt.ac.nz/

Universal College of Learning (Ucol): Palmerston North
http://www.ucol.ac.nz/

Whitireia: Porirua and Wellington
http://www.whitireia.ac.nz/

Nelson Marlborough Institute of Technology
http://www.nmit.ac.nz/

Christchurch Polytechnic Institute of Technology
http://www.cpit.ac.nz

Otago Polytechnic: Dunedin
http://www.otagopolytechnic.ac.nz/

Southern Institute of Technology: Invercargill
http://www.sit.ac.nz/

Wānanga

Te Wānanga o Aotearoa, based in Te Awamutu
www.twoa.ac.nz

Te Wānanga-o-Raukawa, based in Ōtaki
http://www.wananga.com/

Te Whare Wānanga o Awanuiārangi, based in Whakatāne
www.wananga.ac.nz

Te Wānanga Takiura (private teacher training college for Māori-medium teachers), based in Auckland,
www.twt.ac.nz

Police and armed services websites

New Zealand Airforce
http://www.defencecareers.mil.nz/air-force

New Zealand Army
http://www.defencecareers.mil.nz/army

New Zealand Navy
http://www.defencecareers.mil.nz/navy

New Zealand Police
http://www.newcops.co.nz/application-process

GLOSSARY

achievement standard: a nationally registered set of learning outcomes and associated assessment criteria related to a subject that is part of the New Zealand Curriculum. Achievement standards are at Levels 1, 2 and 3 on the New Zealand Qualifications Framework (NZQF) and can be assessed as *Not Achieved*, *Achieved*, achieved with *Merit*, or achieved with *Excellence*. Some achievement standards are assessed internally and others externally.

approved subject: a school subject on a list approved for the University Entrance (UE) award. Many university programmes (e.g., in medicine, engineering, business and commerce) require applicants to have completed one or more of the specified subjects on the approved list. Not all subjects offered by secondary schools are on the approved list.

bachelor's degree: a qualification that normally requires the equivalent of at least three years' full-time study. Bachelors' degrees are taught at universities, polytechnics, whare wānanga and private training establishments.

career guidance counsellor / careers teacher: a member of staff at a school who advises students on study options and career pathways.

compulsory subject: a subject that all students at a school, or those at a particular year level, are required to take.

core subject: those subjects considered to be central to school students' studies, particularly English, mathematics and science.

credit: a numerical value (or points) assigned to standards that represents the estimated time needed for a typical learner to demonstrate that all specified outcomes have been met. It should take around 10 hours per credit (including class time, independent study and time spent in assessment) to meet the requirements of a standard.

dean: a member of staff at a secondary school with responsibilities for students, which may include discipline, administration, pastoral care and course placement.

external assessment: conducted once a year, by specially appointed examiners, through national examinations sat in November and December. A few subjects, such as graphics and art, require students to submit a portfolio of work.

internal assessment: conducted throughout the year, by class teachers, within the school. All unit standards and some achievement standards are internally assessed.

level: there are 10 levels on the New Zealand Qualifications Framework. NCEA qualifications and achievement standards are at levels 1 to 3. (Levels 4 to 6 include advanced trades, technical and business qualifications; Levels 7 to 10 include degrees, graduate and postgraduate qualifications.)

National Certificate: a qualification on the New Zealand Qualifications Framework made up of unit standards in a particular area, such as business administration or animal care. National Certificates are usually registered between Levels 1 and 4, and require a minimum of 40 credits. Credits gained for a National Certificate can also be counted towards NCEA.

New Zealand Qualifications Authority (NZQA): NZQA's primary function is to co-ordinate the administration and quality assurance of national qualifications in New Zealand. NZQA administers the New Zealand Qualifications Framework (including NCEA), runs national senior secondary school examinations, registers and monitors private providers of education and training to ensure they meet quality standards, and evaluates overseas qualifications for people who want their qualification recognised in New Zealand.

New Zealand Qualifications Framework (NZQF): NZQF is administered by the New Zealand Qualifications Authority and contains a comprehensive list of all quality-assured qualifications in New Zealand (worth 40 credits or more).

private training establishment (PTE): a non-state-owned organisation, registered with NZQA, that provides post-school education and training.

reassessment: schools have the choice of offering students who have failed to achieve an internally assessed standard a reassessment opportunity for this standard. This is sometimes referred to as a "re-sit".

Record of Achievement (RoA): an individual student's transcript of standards and credits gained and national qualifications completed, provided by NZQA from a national database.

tertiary education: post-secondary education. This includes learning undertaken in the workplace as well as with providers such as polytechnics, universities, wānanga and private training establishments.

unit standard: originally developed to assess workplace learning, unit standards were subsequently used for conventional school subjects (until 2010). With few exceptions (such as the specific numeracy and literacy unit standards), unit standards will not be used for secondary school curriculum subjects after 2011. Unit standards are assessed internally and, with few exceptions, can only be assessed as *Achieved* or *Not Achieved*.

year co-ordinator: an administrative position in some secondary schools with responsibilities for a particular year level, especially in relation to timetabling of courses and changes in subject choices. Also known as a *level co-ordinator*.

year level: school students move from Year 0 or 1 through to Year 13. Secondary schools teach Years 9 to 13, and students usually work towards NCEA Level 1 in Year 11, NCEA Level 2 in Year 12, and NCEA Level 3 in Year 13.

Uni bound?

Students' Stories of Transition from School to University
Edited by Irena Madjar and Elizabeth McKinley

There is nothing like a good story to capture the imagination and help us engage with other people's experiences. This book is made up of fifteen such stories, written by young New Zealanders as they look back on their individual journeys from school to tertiary education. They come from rural and urban schools located mostly in economically disadvantaged communities, and many are the first in their family to embark on university studies. The authors reflect the ethnic mix of Aotearoa New Zealand today – with Māori, Pacific, European/Pākehā, and other voices telling of their dreams, experiences, and lessons learned along the way. If you are a high school student planning to go to university (or wondering if you should), or a teacher, parent or mentor to a young person in this situation, then this book will give you some helpful pointers.

NZCER Press ISBN 978-1-877398-59-9 RRP: $29.95

Available from: **The New Zealand Council for Educational Research**
PO Box 3237, Wellington 6140, New Zealand

Order from: **NZCER Sales**
Email: **sales@nzcer.org.nz**
Fax: **64 4 384 7933**
Online: **www.nzcer.org.nz**

NZCER PRESS